Wives
of the
Signers

Wives of the Signers

The women behind the
Declaration of Independence

Foreword by David Barton

Aledo, Texas
www.wallbuilders.com

Wives of the Signers: The Women Behind the Declaration of Independence
Excerpted from *The Pioneer Mothers of America*, originally published in 1912.
Reprinted in 1997, WallBuilder Press
Fourth Printing, 2010

Additional materials available from:
WallBuilders
P.O. Box 397
Aledo, TX 76008
(817) 441-6044
www.wallbuilders.com

Cover Painting:
Abigail Adams, courtesy of the Massachusetts Historical Society

Cover Design:
Jeremiah Pent
Lincoln-Jackson
838 Walden Drive
Franklin, TN 37064

ISBN-10: 0-925279-60-9
ISBN-13: 978-0-925279-60-6

Printed in the United States of America

Foreword

The indispensable contributions of women during the American Revolution have received far too little attention from historians. Yet, their contributions were not always overlooked. In fact, signer of the Declaration of Independence Benjamin Rush accurately noted, "The women of America have at last become principals in the glorious American controversy. Their opinions alone and their transcendent influence in society and families must lead us on to success and victory." The life of Abigail Adams (wife of John Adams and mother of John Quincy Adams) provides just such proof.

In the year 1775, war raged around her Bostonian home. John Quincy described that time as "the space of twelve months [in which] my mother, with her infant children, dwelt, liable every hour of the day and the night, to be butchered in cold blood." Courageously facing those dangers, Abigail inculcated patriotism in her children. John Quincy recalled, "My mother was the daughter of a Christian clergyman, and therefore bred in the faith of deliberate detestation of War. . . . Yet, in that same spring and summer of 1775, she taught me to repeat daily, after the Lord's Prayer, and before rising from bed, the *Ode of Collins* on the patriot warriors." John Quincy Adams learned from Abigail that a strong faith in Divine Providence is not incompatible with fighting for one's liberties.

The Adams home also served as a gathering place for minutemen. Even in his latter years, John Quincy still recalled the lessons of patriotism he had learned during those occasions. He recounted that the minutemen once assembled in the family kitchen where there were "some dozen or two of pewter spoons; and I well recollect going into the kitchen and seeing some of the men engaged in running those spoons into bullets for the use of the troops! Do you wonder that a boy of seven years of age, who witnessed this scene, should be a patriot?"

Abigail further displayed her character and courage in 1778, when John was sent overseas by the Congress as a diplomat. It would be three long years before Abigail would reunite with her husband. Noted historian George Bancroft reports that, during that time, Abigail "was charged with the sole care of their little brood of children; managing their farm; keeping house with frugality, opening her doors to the houseless and giving with good will a part of her scant portion to the poor; seeking work for her own hands, and learning French through with the aid of books alone." (Notice how Abigail's life parallels the virtuous woman found in Proverbs 31:10-31). Yet, this self-educated and highly-accomplished woman, the first woman to live in the White House, was completely content to remain in obscurity, satisfied with the praises of her family.

The purpose of *Wives of the Signers* is to highlight the heroines of the American Revolution – heroines like Abigail Adams. These women, although not pledging their "lives, fortunes, and sacred honor" in writing, nevertheless willingly sacrificed all for their country, their families, and their posterity. We are that posterity, enjoying the benefits of their sacrifices. Now, with *Wives of the Signers,* we may finally enjoy the accounts of those women who stood alongside their husbands in creating this great nation.

David Barton
August 1997

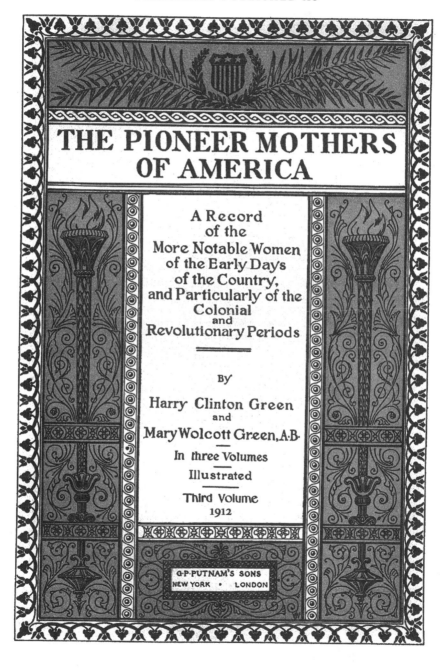

THE PIONEER MOTHERS OF AMERICA

A Record
of the
More Notable Women
of the Early Days
of the Country,
and Particularly of the
Colonial
and
Revolutionary Periods

By

Harry Clinton Green
and

Mary Wolcott Green, A.B.

In three Volumes

Illustrated

Third Volume
1912

G·P·PUTNAM'S SONS
NEW YORK · LONDON

Contents

Illustrations

THE SIGNER

*F*OR *in that hour of Destiny,*
Which tried the men of bravest stock,[1]
He knew the end alone must be
A free land or a traitor's block.

. . . .

Not for their hearths and homes alone,
But for the world their work was done;
On all the winds their thought has flown
Through all the circuit of the sun.

Whittier.

Chapter I

Wives of the Signers

A devoted band of patriotic women who shared the outlawry their husbands had brought upon themselves by declaring their independence of British rule—Many of them suffered bitter persecution from British and Tories—Mary Bartlett forced to fly with her family from her burning home—Elizabeth Adams compelled to resort to needle-work to support her family—Elizabeth Lewis, imprisoned for months, suffered privations and hardships that led to her death—Mary Morris (N. Y.) driven from a beautiful home, wantonly devastated—Annis Stockton, a homeless refugee after the British looted and burned her home—Deborah Hart, driven from her home, saw her husband hunted for months as a criminal and came to her own death from exposure and anxiety.

HISTORY has been generous in its recognition of the patriotism of the men who, on that hot July day in Philadelphia in 1776, pledged their lives, their fortunes, and their sacred honour to uphold and support the Declaration of Independence of all foreign rule. Through that act, these men "put their necks in the halter as traitors" to the British Government, and from John Hancock to George Walton had no other prospect

3

but ignominious death should the struggle for independence prove unsuccessful.

From the day that Declaration was published, these men were proscribed outlaws. Their names were read in every British camp and every British soldier and Tory adherent were taught that they were beyond the pale of consideration as mere military enemies and that they and their families were to be persecuted as dangerous criminals. As opportunity gave, this policy of persecution was duly carried out, and any signer who fell into the hands of the enemy was treated with marked cruelty. A price was set on the heads of John Hancock and Samuel Adams. Dr. Josiah Bartlett was burned out of house and home and his family forced to seek safety by flight. Francis Lewis of New York was reduced to absolute want, his wife imprisoned for months "without a bed or even a change of clothing," eventually dying from the exposure and other hardships she had suffered. Richard Stockton, one of the wealthiest men in New Jersey, died from the treatment he received in prison and his family, which had been harassed and annoyed for years, was left broken and impoverished. "Honest John" Hart, of the same

The Announcement of the Declaration of Independence at the State House, Philadelphia.

State, was hunted like a criminal for months during which time he rarely slept the second night under the same roof and his wife died from the exposure and anxiety. George Clymer of Pennsylvania was almost as obnoxious to the British as Hancock or Adams. He was driven with his family from Philadelphia to Chester County, where the British plundered his house, destroyed his property and forced his family to fly by night for safety. Thomas Nelson of Virginia wrecked health and fortune for the cause, and his family suffered accordingly. Frequent attempts were made to capture Thomas Jefferson, and the untimely death of his wife was hastened, if not caused, by the shock and anxiety she underwent. Thomas Heyward of South Carolina was wounded in battle and saw his property confiscated or destroyed and his family driven from home. These are a few of many instances which are a part of history.

It cost something to be a signer and we do well to honour the men who accepted the responsibility of being in the vanguard of the struggle. It is well to bear in mind, however, that the sacrifices, the dangers, and the hardships

endured by the signers fell with almost equal
weight on their wives and families. Not all of
them, of course, were called upon to face personal
danger or suffer actual physical hardships or
exposure. Many of the members of the Continental Congress who signed the Declaration
were so situated that their families were removed
beyond the reach of the enemy's armies. But
always there was the Tory neighbour, sneaking,
spying, informing, plotting mischief, and often
more to be dreaded than the uniformed enemy
in the open. Always there was the anxiety
over the absent ones; always that lurking distrust
and fear of their great and powerful but pitiless
foe.

All these signers suffered pecuniary losses
because of their connection with the cause,
some of them being brought to the brink of
financial ruin. Such troubles must have fallen
heavily upon the women of the household,
yet rarely a complaint do we find in their correspondence. On the other hand, the letters
and other recorded utterances of the wives of
the signers breathe the utmost devotion not only
to their husbands but to the great cause for
which their husbands had thrown life and fortune

in the balance. In writing of these women individually, considerable difficulty has been encountered because of a lack of authentic data. No publication exists giving even cursory records of them, and in the published lives of the signers but few allusions are made to their wives and families. Consequently the sketches of some of these women of whom we would know more, must necessarily seem unduly brief and meagre in fact and detail. This must be attributed in part to the long lapse of years in which we, as a people, were strangely indifferent to the importance of preserving family records and traditions, and in part to the idea, seemingly so prevalent in the eighteenth century, that the man was not only the head of the family but that he was the family. An instance of this is found in the family Bible of Robert Morris, where it is set down in the handwriting of the great financier himself: "March 2, 1769, Robert Morris married Mary." Fortunately for the historian and genealogist, the White family, of which she was so distinguished a member, had a family Bible of its own.

In considering the wives of the signers, we shall take them according to the roll call of the

States in the Continental Congress, which, beginning with New Hampshire, the northernmost State, gave to Dr. Josiah Bartlett the first vote.

Mary Bartlett

"The wife of Governor Bartlett, the signer, was Mary Bartlett (a cousin), of Newton, N. H., a lady of excellent character and an ornament to society.   She died in 1789," wrote Levi Bartlett, a descendant of the signer, nearly a century after her death.

Not much more of her youth than this can be told.   Her father, Joseph Bartlett, was a soldier at Haverhill, in 1707, where he was made captive by the French and Indians, carried to Canada and held four years.[2]   Mary Bartlett was one of ten children born to Joseph Bartlett, and she was married to her cousin, Josiah Bartlett, in January, 1754.   He was a rising young physician at the time, in the town of Kingston, N. H., and had already attracted favourable attention by reason of his success in the treatment of a throat distemper, known as the "black canker," which had broken out with uncommon virulence.   Mary Bartlett was then twenty-four years old, an amiable girl, well grown and, for the times, well educated. For the next ten years, her life was that of the wife of a popular and prosperous young country doctor. His skill as a practitioner was accepted. He was democratic, kindly, and fast growing in the esteem of his fellow citizens. Always a man of strict integrity, sound judgment, and marked public spirit, he early began to take an active part in public affairs. He was made a civil magistrate and soon after given command of a regiment of militia. In 1765, he was chosen representative to the Provincial Legislature from Kingston. Though Governor Wentworth had appointed him to several positions of honour and profit, Dr. Bartlett felt called upon, almost from the first, to oppose vigorously some of the Governor's measures in the Legislature especially those pertaining to the land grants, a vast system of official peculation that was one of the great evils of the administrations of both the Wentworths. By 1774, the aggressions of the Governor, and the policy of the British Ministry which he was trying to carry out, had grown so burdensome to the people that Dr. Bartlett and a few other leaders found themselves in almost open opposition. He was still a member of the Legislature and in that year we find him at the head of a "Committee of Correspondence," which was in constant communication with Samuel Adams and other patriots of Massachusetts and Connecticut. Then Dr. Bartlett was elected delegate to "a general congress to be held in Philadelphia." This brought down upon him the wrath of Governor Wentworth and his Tory adherents. His appointment as Justice of the Peace was revoked and his commission as Colonel of militia was taken from him. Soon afterward his house was set on fire and burned to the ground, after he had received warning to cease his "pernicious activity."

During all this period, Mary Bartlett had been the closest friend and counsellor of her husband. Just as he had consulted her over his troubles as a young physician, helping to bear the home burdens of his patients and personal friends in their little community, so now he consulted her about the greater troubles and dangers that menaced the country. And always she was the true helpmeet, always the ready and sympathetic friend and judicious adviser. Her patriotism was as ardent as his and burned with as steady a flame, and when

their home lay in ruins and the family were
driven to seek shelter and safety elsewhere,
she took their numerous brood and retired to
their little farm, which she managed thereafter,
leaving him free to devote himself almost entirely to the public business. Between these
public duties Dr. Bartlett found time to rebuild,
on the site of his ruined home, a fine old-style
New England mansion, that still stands. In
all her letters to her husband and her children,
there is not one word of regret at his course
or pity for herself, left alone to bear the double
duties incumbent upon her; no complaints, only
a spirit of loving, helpful sympathy in all his
acts.

Mrs. Bartlett died in their new house in
Kingston, in July, 1789, and her death was a
great blow to her husband, who was at the
time Chief Justice. The following year he was
chosen President of New Hampshire, which office
he held until 1793, when he was elected Governor,
the first the Commonwealth ever had as an
independent State. He declined re-election and
died shortly afterward in the sixty-sixth year
of his age, broken down, according to his own
declaration, by grief and the double duties and

responsibilities imposed upon him since her death.

Twelve children were born to Dr. and Mrs. Bartlett, of whom eight came to maturity. Three sons, Levi, Joseph, and Ezra, followed in their father's footsteps and became eminent physicians, and all three of them took considerable interest in public affairs, holding not a few positions of honour and responsibility. Of the daughters, Mary, who married Jonathan Greeley, Miriam, who married Joseph Calef, Rhoda, who married Reuben True, and Sarah, who married Dr. Amos Gale, were the only ones to leave descendants.

Katharine Moffat Whipple

Captain William Whipple, the second of the New Hampshire delegation to the Continental Congress of 1776, like his confrère, Dr. Josiah Bartlett, married his own cousin. The family records are barren in detail of this union between Katharine Moffat, daughter of Hon. John and Katharine Cutt Moffat, and William Whipple, son of Captain William and Mary Cutt Whipple, but as their mutual ancestors, the Cutts, were among the wealthiest and most prominent

people of the Province, and her father had held
high position in the Provincial government,
she was of good birth and breeding and must
have been of high social standing.

William Whipple, born in 1730, had followed
the sea from the time he shipped as a cabin boy
in his fourteenth year until he retired, in 1759,
in order to enter the mercantile business in
Portsmouth with his brother. William Whipple
had come to command his own ship, while following the sea, and had amassed a considerable
fortune in the West India trade. The mercantile venture at Portsmouth was also prosperous and Captain Whipple continued it until
1775, when he closed out all his business interests
in order to devote himself entirely to public
affairs.

Mrs. Whipple and her husband lived in Portsmouth between the years of their marriage
and the Revolution, but we know little of their
private life. Her portrait was painted by
Copley during this period and is now in possession of Rev. Dr. A. P. Peabody of Cambridge.
One child was born to Captain and Mrs. Whipple,
a daughter who died in infancy. After the death
of this daughter, in the early sixties, Mrs. Whip-

ple adopted a niece, Mary Tufton Moffat, who lived with her uncle and aunt until she grew up and married Nathaniel Appleton Haven.

Captain Whipple was elected to the Continental Congress of 1775, and again in 1776; was made Brigadier General of New Hampshire troops at Saratoga; co-operated with General Sullivan at the siege of Newport in 1778; returned to Congress again in 1778 and 1779; was financial receiver of New Hampshire in 1782 and 1783, and Judge of the Superior Court in 1784, and until his death in 1785. Mrs. Whipple survived him many years.

Hannah Jack Thornton

Hannah Jack, who married Dr. Matthew Thornton, in 1760, was of Scotch-Irish descent, as was her husband. She was eighteen years old at the time of her marriage to Dr. Thornton, who was himself a man of middle age, having been brought to this country at the age of three years, in 1717, by his father, James Thornton, who settled in Wiscasset, Me. After completing his medical studies, young Thornton removed to Londonderry, N. H., to practice.

Mrs. Thornton was a daughter of Andrew

Jack, who settled near Chester, N. H., prior to 1747, at which time his name appears on the Presbyterian records as warden. He had emigrated to New Hampshire from Londonderry, Ireland, but his family was originally Scotch, as was that of his wife, Mary Morrison.

Dr. Thornton, like Dr. Bartlett, had held appointment as an officer in the State militia and a commission as Justice of the Peace, under Governor Wentworth, and, upon the abdication of that Executive in 1776, he was appointed a member of the provisional government. In September of the same year, he was elected a delegate to the Continental Congress and was permitted to add his signature to the Declaration although that measure had been adopted four months previously. He was again a member of Congress in 1777 and afterwards was a judge of the Superior Court. He died in 1803, having outlived his wife about seventeen years. Both were buried at Thornton's Ferry, N. H.

Five children were born to Dr. and Mrs. Thornton, four of whom grew to maturity. James, born in 1763, was married to Mary Parker, and one of his sons, James Shepard Thornton, had a distinguished career in the U. S.

Navy. The torpedo boat *Thornton* was named
in his honour. Matthew Thornton, the youngest son married Fanny Curtis of Amherst. He
became a prominent lawyer of his native State.
Mary Thornton married Hon. Silas Betton of
Salem, N.H., and Hannah married John McGaw,
of Bedford, N. H.[3]

Dorothy Quincy Hancock

By the accident of being the presiding officer
of the Continental Congress of 1776, John
Hancock was the first man to affix his signature
to the Declaration of Independence and thereby
conferred upon his beautiful Boston bride,
Dorothy Quincy, the honour of being the wife
of the first "signer."

Dorothy Quincy was the youngest of the ten
children of Judge Edmund Quincy. She was
born May 10, 1747, and grew up in the sheltered
environment of a wealthy and well regulated
New England home.

"Carefully reared under a gentle mother's
watchfulness through the early part of her life,
when old enough she was launched in the social
world under more favourable auspices than
usually fall to the lot of a young girl. Cultured

Dorothy Quincy Hancock, Wife of Governor John Hancock.
From the painting by Copley owned by Anne Rose Bowen.

and agreeable, she drew friends and attracted admirers; she won all hearts and a place in society from which nothing could dethrone her. Admired and sought after, Dorothy Quincy steered through the dangerous shoals of high-seasoned compliments to remain a bright, unspoiled beauty, that no flattery could harm."

If this seems a rather perfervid tribute, it must be attributed to the possibly biassed viewpoint of an admiring descendant. Dorothy's mother was Elizabeth Wendell, daughter of Abraham and Katharine DeKay Wendell of New York, an educated and accomplished woman of high character, with a taste for social life and a liking for the society of young people. So it came that the Quincy household, with its bevy of handsome girls, had many visitors. John Adams, a rising young lawyer of Boston at the time, was a frequent caller, and in his diary we find that several times he "had gone over to the house of Justice Quincy and had a talk with him." Adams occasionally mentions Esther Quincy, an elder sister of Dorothy, and also a cousin, Hannah Quincy. Both are described as being "handsome and brilliant girls," given to lively repartee, and the young lawyer

with his badinage met in them his match.
In 1759 is found this entry: "I talked with
Esther about the folly of love, about despising
it, about being above it—pretended to be insensible of tender passions, which made them
laugh." Esther at tne time had a devoted ad-
mirer, Jonathan Sewall, whom she married in
1763. Another sister, Elizabeth, had long been
married to Jonathan Sewall's brother, Samuel.
Sarah Quincy, fifteen years older than Dorothy,
was married to General William Greenleaf. Another sister, Katharine, died unmarried.

John Hancock, the handsome young merchant
who had just succeeded to the great wealth
and business of his uncle, Thomas Hancock,
was, of course, a welcome visitor at the Quincy
home. The son of a highly respected minister
and the grandson of another, young Hancock
had graduated from Harvard College at the age
of seventeen. He had immediately gone into
the counting room of his uncle and had greatly
pleased the old gentleman by his intelligence
and attention to his duties. In 1760, the young
man was sent to England to take charge of the
London end of the business. Here he had a
chance to supplement his education with travel

and acquaintance with men of affairs. He had listened to the debates of Parliament, witnessed the funeral of George II and the coronation of George III, and in many ways come to have a good general knowledge of the English people and their way of thinking. Then he was recalled to America by the death of his uncle, who had left him the bulk of his great estate.

Thus John Hancock at the age of twenty-seven found himself one of the wealthiest men of Massachusetts. From that time he began closing out his commercial interests and devoting himself more and more to public affairs. His first public office was that of selectman of the town of Boston, in which position he served for years. In 1766, he was elected from Boston to the General Assembly, having as colleagues Samuel Adams, James Otis, and Thomas Cushing, able men and patriotic, whose influence was important in Hancock's after life. Hancock was public-spirited, generous, and always ready to go to the assistance of a friend. At one time during the Revolution, it was said that not less than one hundred families were subsisting on his benevolence. His popularity grew with every one except the Governor and his official clique, who held Hancock and Adams responsible for the constantly growing spirit of opposition to the acts of King and Parliament. Consequently when Hancock was elected Speaker of the Assembly of 1767, the Governor vetoed the selection. Shortly before this, Governor Barnard had offered Hancock a commission as Lieutenant in the militia. Hancock, knowing that it was a covert attempt at bribing him, tore up the commission in the presence of many prominent citizens. At the opening of the next session of the Assembly, Hancock was again elected Speaker, and again it was vetoed. Then he was elected a member of the Executive Council, and that was vetoed by the Governor. All this but endeared Hancock to the people. During the few years immediately preceding the Battle of Lexington, the British Government was constantly and apprehensively watching Hancock and Adams. They were regarded as dangerous men. They could not be frightened, bribed, nor cajoled. In 1774, the Provincial Congress of Massachusetts unanimously elected John Hancock as its President. "This is the foulest, subtlest, and most venomous serpent ever issued from the egg of sedition. It is the source of rebellion," writes one loyalist pamphleteer of the period.

All this time, John Hancock was courting the handsome daughter of Judge Quincy. Her father was an earnest patriot and their home, from which the mother had departed in 1769, was the gathering place for such men as Samuel and John Adams, Dr. Joseph Warren, James Otis, and others of their rebellious group. John Hancock probably seemed very much of a hero in the eyes of the young woman. Anyway, we are told that she was as enthusiastic a patriot as her lover and entered keenly into their plans and consultations.

John Hancock at this time was living with his aunt, Lydia Hancock, and for safety had removed from Boston to the old Hancock homestead in Lexington, a relative, the Rev. James Clark, living in the same house. Early in 1775, Judge Quincy was called away from home on business and Mistress Dorothy, being left alone in their Boston home, accepted an invitation from Lydia Hancock to pay her a visit, and that is how Dorothy Quincy came to be present at the Battle of Lexington.

The Boston authorities, acting on advice from Great Britain, decided to take Hancock and Adams into custody, and it was arranged to arrest them at the home of Hancock, in Lexington, where they had been staying for several nights. They had been chosen as delegates to the Continental Congress and expected arrest at any time if their whereabouts were known. Through their spies the authorities had learned where Hancock and Adams were staying. They had also learned that a considerable quantity of ammunition and other stores had been gathered at Lexington. Elbridge Gerry had already warned Hancock and Adams to remain constantly on their guard. On April 18th, General Gage ordered the march to Concord. It was then that Dr. Joseph Warren hastily despatched Paul Revere on the ride that has made his name immortal. About midnight, Revere galloped up to the Rev. Mr. Clark's house, which he found guarded by eight men under a sergeant who halted him with the order not "to make so much noise."

"Noise!" exclaimed the excited Revere. "You'll have noise enough before long. The regulars are coming out!"

A window on the second floor was raised and a voice came down: "What is it, courier Revere? We are not afraid of you." It was John Hancock himself and Revere delivered his message.

"Ring the bell!" ordered Hancock, and the bell soon began pealing and continued all night. By daybreak, one hundred and fifty men had mustered for the defence. John Hancock, with gun and sword, prepared to go out and fight with the minute-men, but Adams checked him:

"That is not our business; we belong to the cabinet." Hancock was loath to accept this, but finally saw the wisdom of Adams's decision and went with him, back through the rear of the house and garden to a thickly wooded hill where they could watch the progress of events.

Dorothy Quincy and Aunt Lydia remained in the house, as no danger was apprehended there, and so by chance were eye witnesses of the first battle of the Revolution. Dorothy watched the fray from her bedroom window and in her narration of it notes: "Two men are being brought into the house. One, whose head has been grazed by a ball, insisted that he was dead, but the other, who was shot through the arm, behaved better."

Hancock and Adams retired from their resting place in the woods to the home of Rev. Mr. Merritt in what is now Burlington, and later removed to Bellerica where they lodged in the house of Amos Wyman until they were ready to proceed to Philadelphia.

It is said that John Hancock and the fair Dorothy had a little disagreement following the Battle of Lexington, just before he started for the Pennsylvania capital. The lady, somewhat unstrung by the events of the day, announced her intention of returning to her father's home in Boston. Hancock, who realised the disordered and unsafe condition of the city, refused to allow this. "No, madam," he said, "you shall not return as long as a British bayonet remains in Boston."

"Recollect, Mr. Hancock," she replied with vehemence, "I am not under your authority yet. I shall go to my father's to-morrow."

Next day, however, Aunt Lydia smoothed down the ruffled plumage of the little lady and it was many months before she again saw Boston, and when she went back it was as John Hancock's wife.

A few days after the Battle of Lexington, Dorothy and Aunt Lydia Hancock left the residence of Rev. James Clark and went to Fairfield, Conn., where they were to remain for an indefinite period as the guests of Rev. Thaddeus Burr, a leading citizen. There John Hancock and Dorothy Quincy were married on August 23, 1775, by the Rev. Andrew Elliott. They left at once for Philadelphia, by way of New York, arriving September 5th.

John Adams, in writing of the marriage, says: "His choice was very natural, a granddaughter of the great patron and most revered friend of his father. Beauty, politeness, and every domestic virtue justified his predilection."

Hancock was very much in love with his wife. Notwithstanding his many duties as President of the Continental Congress and other public positions, he wrote to her with great frequency when they chanced to be separated, and always with affection and respect, before and after marriage, and in nearly all of his letters he complains because she does not write to him.

The winter Martha Washington spent in Cambridge, she and Mrs. Hancock became warm friends, exchanging frequent visits. It

was on the occasion of these informal calls that
the wife of the soldier is credited with the somewhat feline remark: "There is a great differ-
ence in our situations. Your husband is in the
cabinet, but mine is on the battlefield."

John Hancock's position during the Revolution as President of Congress and later as
Governor, brought many calls upon both his
hospitality and his benevolence. The generosity
that marked him as a young man characterised
all his career, and his wife entered as heartily
into his benefactions as she did his hospitality.
After the Revolution, they entertained many
people of prominence, as La Fayette, Count
D'Estaing, the French Admiral, Prince Edward
of England, and many others. One of Mrs.
Hancock's grandnieces tells an anecdote of the
time when Admiral D'Estaing visited Boston
harbour with his fleet. Governor Hancock invited him to dine on a certain date, with thirty
of his officers. What was the dismay of the
Governor and Mrs. Hancock when the Admiral
accepted the invitation, and accompanied his
acceptance with the request to be allowed to
bring all his officers, including the midshipmen,
which would bring the number of guests to

above a hundred. There was nothing to do but for the Governor to overlook the Frenchman's bad manners and accede to the request. It was upon Mrs. Hancock's resourcefulness, however, that the duty fell hardest, of providing for so many guests in the short time available. The problem was speedily solved with the exception of the item of milk. The Governor's private dairy could not possibly furnish all that was needed, and there was not a place in Boston where such a supply could be obtained. Mrs. Hancock summoned the life guards and bade them milk the cows pasturing on Boston Common, and if any persons complained, to send them to her. This was done and no one objected. Plenty of milk was obtained and the dinner to the Admiral and his officers was a great success.

Count D'Estaing returned the courtesy by a dinner on board his flagship, at which Mrs. Hancock was the guest of honour. By the side of her plate was a large rosette of ribbon which greatly excited her curiosity. As the toasts were about to be drunk, the Admiral's aide, who sat next to Mrs. Hancock, requested her to pull the ribbon on the rosette, which ran down under the table. She did so and was greatly surprised to find that by so doing she had fired a gun, which was responded to by every vessel in the fleet.

Two children were born to Governor and Mrs. Hancock, a daughter who died in infancy, and a son who died in the ninth year of his age. John Hancock died in 1793, and several years later Mrs. Hancock was married to Captain Scott, who had been a friend of her husband. Captain Scott died in 1809, after which his widow lived a retired life in Boston, until her death several years later.

Abigail Smith Adams

A woman, who exercised great and far-reaching influence in her day and generation and that influence always for the greatest good, was Abigail Adams, wife of John Adams of Massachusetts. Always distrusting her own abilities and education, and never realising that she had talent other than that of being a good wife to John Adams and a mother to his children, her letters pulse with life and feeling, while the pedantic, though patriotic, poems, plays, essays, and histories of her friend, Mercy

Mrs. John Adams.

(Abigail Smith.)

From a picture by C. Schessele.

Warren, are relegated to the dusty shelves of the reference libraries.

Abigail's years were not filled with great events, though she lived in a history-making epoch and her life lines were closely interwoven with those who were among the makers of history. It was never given to her to perform deeds of heroism for country or for cause, but her life was always so lived that we feel that she would have gone to the scaffold if necessary with the same quiet, gracious dignity which always characterised her, from the little farm-house at Braintree to the gilded drawing-rooms of the French and English Courts, or to the unfinished parlours of the White House.

The wife of John Adams was born his social superior, according to the conventions of a community founded almost exclusively on motives of religious zeal, and where "the ordinary distinctions of society were in a great degree subverted, and the leaders of the church, though without worldly possessions to boast of, were held highest in honour." She was the daughter of the Rev. William Smith, a Congregationalist minister of Weymouth. Her grandfather was also a minister, and through her veins, on her mother's

side, flowed the blood of the Quincys, as blue as
any in New England. To this mating John
Adams brought nothing but the vigour and
strength of mind and body that had come to the
son of a farmer of limited means but of correct life
and high ideals. He had his profession but little
practice, and the profession itself was not held
in the highest regard by many of the good people
of the day. Still there was no decided opposition,[4] and John and Abigail were married
October 26, 1764, when she was twenty years
old. They went to Braintree to live on his
little farm, for although he was a lawyer of
promise and acknowledged capabilities, his income from his profession must be helped out
by his farm in order that they might live.

Mrs. Adams had but a limited education.
Educational opportunities, especially for women,
were restricted in the early days, and the delicate
condition of her health had always precluded
her being sent from home to acquire even the
common-school training of the day. As she
herself wrote in later years: "My early education did not partake of the abundant opportunities which the present day affords and which
even our common schools now afford. I was

never sent to any school; I was always sick."
Massachusetts, even at that day, ranked high
in point of its educational facilities, but not for
its women. "While the sons of the family
received every possible advantage, compatible
with the means of the father, the daughters'
interests, so far as mental development was
concerned, were ignored. To aid the mother
in manual household labour and by self-denial
and increased industry to forward the welfare
of the brothers, was the most exalted responsibility to which any woman aspired. To
women, there was then no career open, no life
work to perform outside the narrow walls of
home. Every idea of self-culture was swallowed
up in the routine of so-called practical life, and
what knowledge they obtained was from the
society of the learned and the eagerness with
which they treasured up and considered the
conversation of others."

The girl was, however, a great reader and a
voluminous letter-writer. "The women of the
last century," her biographer continues, "were
more remarkable for their letter-writing pro-
pensities than the novel-reading and more
pretentious daughters of this era; their field

was larger and the stirring events of the times
made it an object of more interest. Even
though self-taught, the young ladies of Massachusetts were certainly readers and their taste
was not for the feeble and nerveless sentiments,
but was derived from the deepest wells of
English literature. Almost every house in the
Colony possessed some heirlooms in the shape of
standard books, even if the number was limited
to the Bible and Dictionary. Many, especially
ministers, could display relics of their English
ancestors' intelligence in the libraries handed
down to them, and the study of their contents
was evident in many of the grave correspond-
ences of that early time."

For ten years after they were married, the
current of life moved very smoothly for the
Adams family. Mistress Adams spun and wove,
knitted stockings for her family, looked after
the little farm, and wrote frequent letters to her
girlhood friend, Mrs. Mercy Warren, the gifted
sister of James Otis. Within this time, Abigail
had become the mother of a daughter and three
sons. In 1774, Mr. Adams was one of the
delegates chosen from Massachusetts to confer
with delegates from other Colonies upon matters

of common interest; and in August he accompanied Samuel Adams, Robert Treat Paine, and Thomas Cushing to Philadelphia, where the meeting was held. In two months he was again at home, but in May, 1775, the Congress again met and he returned to Philadelphia, making the long journey on horseback. At Hartford, only five days after he had left home, he received the news of the happenings at Lexington.

That was an eventful year for Mrs. Adams. Bancroft writes of her: "In November, 1775, Abigail Smith, wife of John Adams, was at her home near the foot of Penn Hill charged with the sole care of her little brood of children; managing their farm; keeping house with frugality, though opening her doors to the houseless and giving with good will a part of her scant portion to the poor; seeking work for her own hands and ever busily occupied, now at the spinning-wheel, now making amends for never having been sent to school by learning French, though with the aid of books alone. Since the departure of her husband for Congress, the arrow of death had sped near her by day and the pestilence that walks in darkness had entered her humble mansion. She herself was still

very weak after a violent illness; her house was
a hospital in every part; and such was the distress of the neighbourhood she could hardly
find a well person to look after the sick. Her
youngest son had been rescued from the grave
by her nursing. Her mother had been taken
away and, after the austere manner of her
forefathers, buried without prayer. Winter was
hurrying on; during the days family affairs
took all her attention, but her long evenings,
broken by the sound of the storm on the ocean,
or the enemy's artillery on Boston, were lonesome and melancholy. Ever in the silent night,
ruminating on the love and tenderness of her
departed parent, she needed the consolation
of her husband's presence; but when she read
the King's proclamation she willingly gave up
her nearest friend exclusively to his perilous,
duties and sent him her cheering message:
'This intelligence will make a plain path for
you, though a dangerous one. I could not join
to-day in the petition of our worthy pastor
for a reconciliation between our no longer parent
state but tyrant state and these Colonies. Let
us separate; they are unworthy to be our breth-
ren. Let us renounce them; and instead of

supplications, as formerly, for their prosperity, let us beseech the Almighty to blast their counsels and bring to naught all their devices.' "

In December, Mr. Adams was home again, but only for a few weeks, and in March he was on his way back to Philadelphia. One of her letters to him at this time speaks of the anticipated attack on Boston, and says: "It has been said to-morrow and to-morrow, but when the dreadful to-morrow will be I know not."

"Yet even as she wrote," says her biographer,[5] "the first peal of the American guns rang out their dissonance on the chilling night winds, and the house shook from cellar to garret." It was no time for calm thoughts now, and she left her letter unfinished to go out and watch the lurid lights that flashed and disappeared in the distance. Next morning she walked to Penn Hill where she sat listening to the amazing roar and watching the British shells as they fell around about the camp of her friends. Her home at the foot of the hill was all of her earthly wealth, and the careful husbanding of each year's crop her only income; yet while she ever and anon cast her eye upon it, the thoughts that welled into words were not of selfish repinings,

but of proud expressions of high-souled patriotism. "The cannonade is from our army," she
continues, "and the sight is one of the grandest
in nature, and is of the true species of the
sublime. 'Tis now an incessant roar. To-night
we shall realise more terrible scenes still; I wish
myself with you out of hearing, as I cannot
assist them, but I hope to give you joy of
Boston, even if it is in ruins before I send this
away."

Mr. Adams returned early in the fall, but it
was but a short respite for her loneliness as he
came to announce that he had been chosen to
go to France. At first it was thought that he
could take his wife and little ones with him, but
the manifold dangers of the voyage deterred
him. A small and not very fast vessel had been
secured, and this the British fleet was bent on
capturing, as John Adams was a man with a price
on his head. On every account it was decided
that it would be best for Mr. Adams to go alone,
but he compromised by taking his son, John
Quincy Adams, then eleven years old, and they
sailed in February. Again was Mrs. Adams
left alone to care for her little farm and her
young children, with but little to break the

lonesome monotony but her letters. After an absence of eighteen months Mr. Adams came home, but it was only for a breathing spell, as almost immediately he was sent to Great Britain to negotiate a peace.

To the wife at least the parting seemed the hardest they had yet endured and her heart found relief in the following words: "My habitation, how desolate it looks! my table, I sit down to it, but cannot swallow my food. Oh! why was I born with so much of sensibility, and why possessing it have I so often been called on to struggle with it? Were I sure you would not be gone, I could not withstand the temptation of coming to you, though my heart would suffer over again the cruel torture of separation." In the spring of 1781, Mrs. Adams could stand the separation no longer; some six months before she had written: "I feel unable to sustain even the idea that it will be half that period ere we meet again. Could we live to the age of antediluvians, we might better support this separation, but with threescore years circumscribing the life of man, how painful is the idea that of that short space only a few years of social happiness are our allotted portion!" A few months after

that, she laid her aged father away in the
Boston churchyard beside her mother, and there
was nothing left to hold her away from her
husband except the hardships and perils of a
sea voyage. It was early in 1784 that Mrs.
Adams, accompanied by her daughter, sailed in
the *Active* for England. It was Mrs. Adams's
first sea voyage and she suffered so much
from sea-sickness that she wrote nothing for
the first sixteen days of her voyage—a long time
for Abigail Adams to keep her pen from paper.
From that time her journal is a narrative of
rare interest. Mrs. Adams reached London July
23d, where she was met by her husband and
by her son, John Quincy Adams, whom she
had not seen for six years. The united family
accompanied the father to Paris, where they
took up their residence at Auteuil, not far from
the residence of Dr. Franklin, and where they
resided for a year. Then they removed to
London, Mr. Adams having been appointed
Minister to that country.

"Mrs. Adams, at the age of forty," writes
her biographer, "found herself suddenly trans-
planted into a scene wholly new. From a life
of the utmost retirement in a small and quiet

country town in New England, she was at once
thrown into the busy and bustling scenes of
the populous and wealthy cities of Europe.
Not only was her position novel to herself,
but there had been nothing like it among her
countrywomen. She was the first representative of her sex from the United States at the
Court of Great Britain. The impressions made
upon her mind were, therefore, uncommonly
open and free from the restraints which an established routine of precedents is apt to create.
Her residence in France during the first of her
European experience appears to have been much
enjoyed, notwithstanding the embarrassment felt
by her from not speaking the language. That
in England, which lasted three years, was somewhat affected by the temper of the sovereign.
George and his Queen could not get over the
mortification attending the loss of the American
Colonies, nor at all times suppress the manifes-
tation of it, when the presence of their Minister
forced the subject on their recollection."

In one of the many letters which she was
constantly writing to her sister or her daughter,
Mrs. Adams refers to this in a way, though it is
rare that the good woman allows herself to show

that much ill feeling. It was at the time when, in consequence of the French Revolution, the throne of England was thought to be in danger, she wrote "with regret for the country but without sympathy for the Queen. Humiliation for Charlotte is no sorrow for me; she richly deserves her full portion for the contempt and scorn which she took pains to discover."

Mr. Adams returned to America with his family in the summer of 1788. The government was organised under its present Constitution in April of the following year, and he was elected Vice-President and established his home in New York. In a letter to her sister, Mrs. Adams writes that she "would return to Braintree during the recess of Congress, but the season of the year renders the attempt impracticable." In her letter she speaks of Mrs. Washington's "drawing-rooms" and tells of the many invitations to entertainments she receives, but that her own delicate health and the illness of her son prevent her going much into society. After a year's residence in New York, the Adamses removed, with the seat of government, to Philadelphia. She still called the little farmhouse at Braintree, home, and visited there a portion of every year. It was from Braintree that she wrote in February, 1797, to President Adams, as he succeeded Washington:

> "The sun is dressed in brightest beams
> To give thy honours to the day.

And may it prove an auspicious prelude to each ensuing season. You have this day to declare yourself head of a nation. 'And now, O Lord my God, thou hast made thy servant ruler over the people; give him an understanding heart, that he may know how to go out and come in before this great people; that he may discern between good and bad. For who is able to judge this thy so great people'; were words of a royal sovereign and not less applicable to him who is invested with the Chief Magistracy of a nation, though he wear not a crown nor the robes of royalty. My thoughts and my meditations are with you, though personally absent; and my petitions to Heaven are that 'the things that make for peace may not be hidden from your eye.' My feelings are not those of pride or ostentation upon this occasion. They are solemnised by a sense of the obligations, the important trusts, and numerous duties

connected with it. That you may be enabled
to discharge them with honour to yourself,
with justice and impartiality to your country,
and with satisfaction to this great people shall
be the daily prayer of your——"

In June, 1800, the Federal Government was
removed to Washington where in January, 1801,
Mrs. Adams presided at the first New Year's
reception ever given at the White House,
keeping up the formal etiquette established by
Mrs. Washington in New York and Philadelphia.
In that year, Mrs. Adams's health began to fail
and the necessity of the bracing climate of her old
home as well as a desire to look after Mr. Adams's
little property led her to spend much of her time
in Massachusetts. One of her biographers has
said of her career in Washington: "She lived in
Washington only four months—and yet she is in-
separably connected with it. She was mistress of
the White House less than half a year, but she
stamped it with her individuality and none have
lived there since who have not looked upon her as
the model and guide. It is not asserting too much
to say that the first occupant of that historic house
stands without a rival, and receives a meed of
praise awarded to no other American woman."

A few days after Mrs. Adams became mistress of the White House, she wrote the following letter to her daughter, Mrs. Smith:

"Washington, November 21, 1800.

"My Dear Child:

"I arrived here on Sunday last, and without meeting with any accident worth noticing, except losing ourselves when we left Baltimore, and going eight or nine miles on the Frederick road, by which means we were obliged to go the other eight through woods, where we wandered two hours without finding a guide or the path. Fortunately, a straggling black came up with us, and we engaged him as a guide to extricate us out of our difficulty. But woods are all you see from Baltimore until you reach the city,— which is only so in name. Here and there is a small cot, without a glass window, interspersed amongst the forests, through which you travel miles without seeing any human being. In the city there are buildings enough, if they were compact and finished, to accommodate Congress and those attached to it: but as they are, and scattered as they are, I see no great comfort for them. The river, which runs up to Alex-

andria, is in full view of my window, and I see
the vessels as they pass and repass. The house
is upon a grand and superb scale, requiring
about thirty servants to attend and keep the
apartments in proper order, and perform the
ordinary business of the house and stables:
an establishment very well proportioned to the
President's salary. The light in the apartments
from the kitchen to parlours and chambers, is a
tax indeed; daily agues, is another very cheering comfort. To assist us in this great castle,
and render less attendance necessary, bells are
wholly wanting, not one single one being hung
through the whole house, and promises are all
you can obtain. This is so great an inconveni-
ence, that I know not what to do, or how to do.
The ladies from Georgetown and in the city have
many of them visited me. Yesterday I returned
fifteen visits,—but such a place as Georgetown
appears,—why our Milton is beautiful. But no
comparisons;—if they will put me up some bells,
and let me have wood enough to keep fires, I
design to be pleased. I could content myself
almost anywhere three months; but surrounded
with forest, can you believe that wood is not to
be had, because people cannot be found to cut

and cart it? Briesler entered into a contract
with a man to supply him with wood; a small
part, a few cords only, has he been able to get.
Most of that was expended to dry the walls of
the house before we came in, and yesterday the
man told him it was impossible for him to
procure it to be cut and carted. He has had
recourse to coals; but we cannot get grates
made and set. We have indeed come into a
new country.

"You must keep all this to yourself, and
when asked how I like it, say that I write you
the situation is beautiful, which is true. The
house is made habitable, but there is not a
single apartment finished, and all withinside,
except the plastering, has been done since
Briesler came. We have not the least fence-
yard, or other convenience, without, and the
great unfinished audience room I make a drying-
room of, to hang up the clothes in. The principal
stairs are not up, and will not be this winter.
Six chambers are made comfortable; two are
occupied by the President and Mr. Shaw; two
lower rooms, one for a common parlour and one
for a levee room. Upstairs there is the oval
room, which is designed for the drawing-room,

and has the crimson furniture in it. It is a very handsome room now, but when completed will be beautiful. If the twelve years, in which this place has been considered as the future seat of government, had been improved, as they would have been if in New England, very many of the present inconveniences would have been removed. It is a beautiful spot, capable of every improvement, and the more I view it, the more I am delighted with it. Since I sat down to write, I have been called down to a servant from Mount Vernon, with a billet from Major Custis, and a haunch of venison, and a kind, congratulatory letter from Mrs. Lewis, upon my arrival in the city, with Mrs. Washington's love, inviting me to Mount Vernon, where, health permitting, I will go, before I leave this place. . . . Two articles are much distressed for: the one is bells, but the more important one is wood. Yet you cannot see wood for the trees. No arrangement has been made, but by promises never performed, to supply the newcomers with fuel. Of the promises, Briesler had received his full share. He had procured nine cords of wood: between six and seven of that was kindly burnt up to dry the walls of the house, which

ought to have been done by the commissioners,
but which, if left to them, would have remained
undone to this day. Congress poured in, but.
shiver, shiver. No wood-cutters nor carters to
be had at any rate. We are now indebted to
a Pennsylvania waggon to bring us, through the
first clerk in the Treasury Office, one cord and a.
half of wood, which is all we have for this house,.
where twelve fires are constantly required and
where, we are told, the roads will soon be so
bad that it cannot be drawn. Briesler procured
two hundred bushels of coal, or we must have
suffered. This is the situation of almost every
other person. The public officers have sent to
Philadelphia for wood cutters and waggons.

"The vessel which has my clothes and other
matters is not arrived. The ladies are impatient.
for a drawing-room: I have no looking-glasses,
but dwarfs, for this house; not a twentieth part.
lamps enough to light it. Many things were
stolen, many are broken by the removal;
amongst the number, my tea-china is more than
half missing. Georgetown affords nothing. My
rooms are very pleasant and warm, whilst the
doors of the hall are closed.

"You can scarce believe that here, in this.

wilderness-city, I should find myself so occupied
as it is. My visitors—some of them come three
or four miles. The return of one of them is the
work of one day. Most of the ladies reside in
Georgetown, or in scattered parts of the city,
at two and three miles' distance. We have all
been very well as yet; if we can by any means
get wood, we shall not let our fires go out, but
it is at a price indeed; from four dollars it has
risen to nine. Some say it will fall, but there
must be more industry than is to be found here
to bring half enough to the market for the consumption of the inhabitants."

The remainder of her life, 1801 to 1818, Mrs.
Adams lived almost uninterruptedly at Quincy
and her declining years were marked with that
cheerfulness and dignity that were ever her
dominant characteristics. She retained her
faculties to the last and as one who knew
her well, said: "Her sunny spirit enlivened
the small social circle around her, brightened the
solitary hours of her husband, and spread the
influence of her example over the town where
she lived." To her granddaughter she wrote
October 26, 1814: "Yesterday completes half

a century since I entered the marriage state, then just your age. I have great cause of thankfulness that I have lived so long and enjoyed so large a portion of happiness as has been my lot. The greatest source of unhappiness I have known in that period has arisen from the long and cruel separations which I was called, in a time of war, and with a young family around me, to submit to."

Mrs. Adams died of an attack of fever, October 26, 1818, in the seventy-fifth year of her age, and was laid at rest in the Congregational church of Quincy, where eight years later her eminent husband was laid beside her. Over their last resting place has been placed a marble slab with an inscription prepared by their eldest son, John Quincy Adams.

Thus passed away one of the most remarkable and interesting women of the Revolutionary period. "To learning, in the ordinary acceptance of that term," writes her grandson, "Mrs. Adams could make no claim. Her reading had been extensive in the lighter departments of literature and she was well acquainted with the poets of her own language, but it went no further. It is the soul shining through the words that gives them their greatest attraction; the spirit ever equal to the occasion, whether a great or a small one; a spirit inquisitive and earnest in the little details of life, as when in France or England; playful when she describes daily duties, but rising to the call when the roar of the cannon is in her ears—or when she is reproving her husband for not knowing her better than to think her a coward and to fear telling her bad news."

In Randall's *Life of Thomas Jefferson*, the author has given a rarely interesting estimate of the character of Mrs. Adams. Speaking of her in connection with certain letters which she wrote to Mr. Jefferson, the writer says: "We must not judge too harshly of Mrs. Adams, or pronounce her destitute of womanly amiability. Her lofty lineaments carried a trace of the Puritan severity. They were those of the helmed Minerva, and not of the cestus-girdled Venus. Her correspondence uniformly exhibits a didactic personage—a little inclined to assume a sermonising attitude, as befitted the well-trained and self-reliant daughter of a New England country clergyman—and a little inclined, after the custom of her people, to return thanks

Mrs. Robert R. Livingston.

that she had no lot or part in anything that was not of Massachusetts. Perhaps the masculine-ness of her understanding extended somewhat to the firmness of her temper. But towering above and obscuring these minor angularities, she pos-sessed a strength of intellectual and moral char-acter which commands unqualified admiration. Her decision would have manifested itself for her friend or her cause, when softer spirits would have shrunk away, or been paralysed with terror. When her New England frigidness gave way and kindled to enthusiasm, it was not the burning straw but the red-hot steel. On the stranding deck, at the gibbet's foot, in any other deadly pass where undaunted moral courage can light up the coming gloom of 'the valley of the shadow of death,' Mrs. Adams would have stood by the side of those she loved, uttering words of encourage-ment; and in that more desperate pass where death or overthrow are balanced against dishon-our, she would have firmly bade the most loved friends on earth embrace the former like a bride."

Elizabeth Checkley Adams

Elizabeth Checkley, the first wife of Samuel Adams, "Father of the Revolution," was the daughter of Rev. Samuel Checkley, pastor of the New South Church in Boston. The elder Checkley and the father of Samuel Adams were life-long friends, and it is said that it was the influence of the elder Adams that secured the appointment of his friend to the pastorate. Consequently it brought satisfaction to both families when it was found that the young people had plighted their troth. They were married in October, 1749. She was twenty-four years old at the time and, as her daughter has written, "was a rare example of virtue and piety blended with a retiring and modest demeanour and the charms of elegant womanhood."

The families of Adams and Checkley had been connected by marriage in the previous century, Captain John Adams having married Hannah, daughter of Anthony Checkley, first Attorney-General of the Province under the New Charter, and an ancestor of Rev. Samuel Checkley; Elizabeth Checkley's mother, was a Rolfe, daughter of Rev. Benjamin Rolfe, minister at Haverhill, at the time of the "Sack of Haverhill" by the Indians in 1708. In this fighting the minister was killed, together with about one hundred other persons, and many more were carried away. According to Drake's *History of Boston*, a maid-servant in the employ of Rev. Mr. Rolfe saved the two little daughters of the minister by her bravery and presence of mind. She overheard the Indians breaking into the house and, springing from her bed, took the two little girls, Elizabeth and Mary, aged respectively nine and eleven years, and hurried them into the cellar where she secreted them under two large tubs. They were not found, though the savages ransacked the whole house. It was one of these little girls, Elizabeth, who afterward became the wife of Rev. Samuel Checkley, and mother of Elizabeth Checkley who married Samuel Adams.

Five children were born to Samuel and Elizabeth Adams, only two of whom came to maturity, Samuel, Jr., and Hannah. Mrs. Adams died July 25, 1757. After this date in the family Bible there is written, in the hand of Samuel Adams: "To her husband she was as sincere a friend as she was a faithful wife. Her exact economy in all her relative capacities, her kindred on his side as well as her own admire. She ran her Christian race with remarkable steadiness

and finished in triumph! She left two small
children. God grant they may inherit her
graces!"

Elizabeth Wells Adams

Far removed from the brilliant social circle
of which Dorothy Hancock was the bright
particular star, and inferior intellectually to
Abigail Adams, Elizabeth Wells, second wife
of Samuel Adams, was yet a woman of most
excellent qualities and well worthy of being the
helpmeet of that patriot and statesman during
the most trying period of his life.

Samuel Adams's characterisation of Benjamin
Franklin as being "a great philosopher but a
poor politician" might be paraphrased as
applied to himself as being "a great politician
but a very improvident family man." His
whole life was practically given up to public
affairs, while private interests, business, and
family matters were neglected in a way that
would have driven a woman less loyal and even-
tempered than Elizabeth Adams to bitter complaint, if not open rebellion. Yet always we
find her cheerful and sympathetic; always a
faithful and loving wife to Samuel Adams and

a tender mother to his motherless children. His business might be going to ruin through neglect while he talked politics with his neighbours on the street corners, his leaky roof go unshingled while he made patriots of the workmen of the sail-lofts and shipyards of Boston, but not one word of complaint or fault-finding do we hear from his family.

Politics came as natural to Samuel Adams as the air he breathed—not the petty politics that plots and plans for place or patronage, but the great politics that is the practical side of statesmanship; the politics that began by teaching a crude and simple-minded people their inherent rights as freeborn men and women, and building up a spirit of opposition to any encroachments upon those rights, whether foreign or domestic; the politics that finally wrenched a handful of straggling Colonies from a great and powerful monarchy and welded them together into a compact and harmonious republic. Such was the politics of Samuel Adams, and the very thesis that won for him from Harvard College, in 1743, his Master of Arts degree, "Whether it be lawful to resist the Supreme Magistrate, if the Commonwealth cannot be otherwise preserved," shows, not only the bent of his mind, but also, that however much other leaders of revolutionary sentiment may have looked forward to reconciliation with the mother country, on a basis of justice to the Colonies, Samuel Adams, almost from the first, saw nothing ahead but independence.

Samuel Adams was forty-two years old when he married Elizabeth Wells, fifth daughter of his intimate friend, Francis Wells, an English merchant who came to Boston with his family in 1723. She was twenty-nine years old at the time of the marriage. He was not a successful man according to the standard of most of his thrifty neighbours, though looked upon as one of strict integrity and blameless morality. He could not make money and, what was more to his discredit in their eyes, he seemed to have no desire to accumulate property. His father had left him a fairly profitable malting business, a comfortable house on Purchase Street, and one thousand pounds in money. Half the money he had loaned to a friend who never repaid him. The malt business was neglected and mismanaged so that it did not pay expenses. But always and ever, "Sam" Adams, as he was generally known, was talking politics, writing for the newspapers, debating some measure before the town meeting, or framing up some act for the Assembly calculated to strengthen the rights of the people or to awaken opposition to British encroachment.

Boston at that time was a city of about 18,000 inhabitants and noted already as a "reading town." Education was general. Nearly every person read some one of the five newspapers that were published there and they carried columns of announcements from the booksellers. Of news and impersonal articles, such as go to make up the newspapers of our day, there was little. But letters from the people championing various lines of thought, letters that argued, letters that pleaded, letters of vehement invective and insinuating sophistry, letters signed by the writers and letters signed by *nom-de-plume*, filled the columns of the papers and exercised a vast influence on public opinion. Samuel Adams was an indefatigable writer for the newspapers, appearing under many pen names, but always in advocacy of some measure that he was preparing to have the town meeting endorse or the Assembly put through. A Tory writer of the day is quoted

as saying: "The town meeting of Boston is the
hotbed of sedition. It is there that all their
dangerous insurrections are engendered; it is
there that the flame of discord and rebellion is
lighted up and disseminated over the Province."

"In the year 1764," says Hosmer, his biographer,[6] "Samuel Adams had reached the age
of forty-two. Even now his hair was becoming
grey, and a peculiar tremulousness of the head
and hands made it seem as if he were already
on the threshold of old age. His constitution,
nevertheless, was remarkably sound. His frame
of about medium stature was muscular and well
knit. His eyes were a clear steel grey, his nose
prominent, the lower part of his face capable
of great sternness, but in ordinary intercourse
wearing a genial expression. Life had brought
him much of hardship. In 1757 his wife had
died. . . . Misfortune had followed him in
business. The malt house had been an utter
failure; his patrimony had vanished little by
little, so that beyond the mansion on Purchase
Street, with its pleasant harbour view, little
else remained. His house was becoming rusty
through want of means to keep it in repair.
On the sixth of December of this year he married

for his second wife Elizabeth Wells, a woman of efficiency and cheerful fortitude, who, through the forty years of hard and hazardous life that remained to him, walked sturdily at his side. It required indeed no common virtue to do this, for while Samuel Adams superintended the birth of the child Independence, he was quite careless how the table at home was spread, and as to the condition of his own children's clothes and shoes. More than once the family would have become objects of charity if the hands of his wife had not been ready and skilful."

In the present day Samuel Adams would have been called a political "boss." Boston was as absolutely ruled by its "town meeting" as any city of to-day is governed by its mayor and council, and "Town-meeting Sam" Adams was absolute in his direction and control of the town meeting. It was he who outlined policies, made up slates, and saw that they were put through. Always he held some minor office, generally one without a salary attached and entirely out of keeping with his services and the power he exercised. For "Sam" Adams as a boss had his limitations which would have been laughed at by the political bosses of later days.

He remained as poor as ever. No shadow of
corruption ever fell across his path. No political job ever left the taint of graft on his hands.
He was a collector of taxes for years. Times
were hard, money woefully scarce, and the
collections became sadly in arrears. Adams's
enemies raised the cry of defalcation. Then it
came out that Sam Adams had refused to sell
out the last cow or pig or the last sack of
potatoes or corn meal or the scant furniture
of a poor man to secure his taxes. He had told
his superiors in authority that the town did
not need the taxes as badly as most of these
poor people needed their little belongings and
that he would rather lose his office than force
such collections. It was, of course, a poor
showing for an official, but it put Sam Adams
and the plain people of Boston so closely together
that they were ready, ever after, to elect him
to any office that he would accept.

Writing of Adams in 1769, Hosmer says:
"For years now, Samuel Adams had laid aside
all pretence of private business and was devoted
simply and solely to public affairs. The house
on Purchase Street still afforded the family a
home. His sole source of income was the small

salary (one hundred pounds) he received as clerk of the Assembly. His wife, like himself, was contented with poverty; through good management, in spite of their narrow means, a comfortable home life was maintained in which the children grew up happy and in every way well trained and cared for. John Adams tells of a drive taken by these two kinsmen on a beautiful June day, not far from this time, in the neighbourhood of Boston. Then as from the first and ever after there was an affectionate intimacy between them. They often called one another brother, though the relationship was only that of second cousin. 'My brother, Samuel Adams, says he never looked forward in his life; never planned, laid a scheme or formed a design of laying up anything for himself or others after him.' The case of Samuel Adams is almost without a parallel as an instance of enthusiastic, unswerving devotion to public service throughout a long life."

It is not our purpose in these pages to give, even in outline, a history of the great work that Samuel Adams did for the cause of American independence. But in order to gain insight into the character of Elizabeth Adams and show

what the wife had to contend with, the utter
devotion of her husband to the public business
and his singular unselfishness, so far as that
business was concerned, must be dwelt upon.
It is easy enough at this time to see the great
stakes for which Samuel Adams was playing;
to understand his carefully laid plans and to
sympathise with his disinterested patriotism.
But we must remember that Elizabeth Adams,
doing needlework and kitchen gardening to eke
out the scant allowance she had to furnish a
livelihood for herself and family, was looking
at the fabric from the wrong side. What is to
us a strong, harmonious, and beautiful pattern,
must have been to her a motley collection of
ragged ends, thrown together without rhyme
or reason—something dull, distorted, and indis-
cribably ugly. Yet we hear of no complainings
—no chidings because of his thriftless waste
of time and talent working for other people
without compensation and neglecting his own
affairs and family. Always she and his children
seemed to think that whatever he thought or
whatever he did must be right.

During the summer of 1774, Samuel Adams
was a busy man. He was making preparations

to attend the Congress that was to be held in Philadelphia, and was at the head of several committees devoted to the relief of Boston. Owing to the closing of the port, the city was in sadly straitened circumstances. Donations were coming from far and near and were distributed by one of the committees of which Adams was chairman. Another of his committees laid out public works, opening streets and wharves and furnishing work for many citizens. Hosmer, writing of Samuel Adams at this time, says:

"He still occupied the house in Purchase Street, the estate connected with which had, as time went forward, through the carelessness of its preoccupied owner, become narrowed to a scanty tract. . . . Shortly before this time he had been able, probably with the help of friends, to put his home in good order, and managed to be hospitable. For apparently, life went forward in his home, if frugally, not parsimoniously, his admirable wife making it possible for him, from his small income as clerk of the House, to maintain a decent housekeeping. His son, now twenty-two years old, a young man for whom much could be hoped, was studying

medicine with Dr. Warren, after a course at
Harvard. His daughter (Hannah Adams) was
a promising girl of seventeen. With the young
people and their intimates the father was
cordial and genial. He had an ear for music
and a pleasant voice in singing, a practice which
he much enjoyed. The house was strictly religious; grace was said at each meal, and the
Bible is still preserved from which some member
read aloud each night. Old Surry, a slave woman
given to Mrs. Adams in 1765, and who was freed
upon coming into her possession, lived in the
family nearly fifty years, showing devoted
attachment. When slavery was abolished in
Massachusetts, papers of manumission were
made out for her in due form; but these she
threw into the fire in anger, saying she had
lived too long to be trifled with. The servant
boy whom Samuel Adams carefully and kindly
reared, became afterwards a mechanic of character and worked efficiently in his former
master's behalf when at length, in his old age,
Adams was proposed for Governor. Nor must
Queue be forgotten, the big intelligent New-
foundland dog, who appreciated perfectly what
was his due as the dog of Sam Adams. He had

a vast antipathy to the British uniform. He was cut and shot in several places by soldiers, in retaliation for his own sharp attacks, for the patriotic Queue anticipated the 'embattled farmers' of Concord Bridge in inaugurating hostilities, and bore to his grave honourable scars from his fierce encounters."

"Until his fifty-third year, Samuel Adams had never left his native town except for places a few miles distant. The expenses of the journey and the sojourn in Philadelphia were arranged for by the legislative appropriation. But the critical society of a prosperous town and the picked men of the Thirteen Colonies were to be encountered. A certain sumptuousness in living and apparel would be not only fitting but necessary in the deputies, that the great Province which they represented might suffer no dishonour. Samuel Adams himself probably would have been quite satisfied to appear in the old red coat of 1770 in which he had been painted by Copley[7] and which his wife's careful darning doubtless still held together; but his townsmen arranged it differently."

How this arrangement was brought about is told in a private letter written August 11,

1774: "The ultimate wish and desire of the *high* government party is to get Sam Adams out of the way, when they think they may accomplish everyone of their plans; but however some may despise him, he has certainly very many friends. For, not long since, some persons (their names unknown) sent and asked his permission to build him a new barn, the old one being decayed, which was executed in a few days. A second sent to ask leave to repair his house, which was thoroughly effected soon. A third sent to beg the favour of him to call at a tailor's shop and be measured for a suit of clothes and chose his cloth, which was finished and sent home for his acceptance. A fourth presented him with a new wig, a fifth with a new hat, a sixth with six pairs of the best silk hose, a seventh with six pairs of fine thread ditto, an eighth with six pairs of shoes, and a ninth modestly inquired of him whether his finances were not rather low than otherwise. He replied it was true that was the case but he was very indifferent about these matters, so that his *poor* abilities were of any service to the public; upon which the gentleman obliged him to accept of a purse containing about fifteen or twenty Johannes."

The next glimpse we get of the family relations of Samuel and Elizabeth Adams was
in a letter that has been preserved, which
he wrote from Philadelphia, June 28, 1775,
nearly a year after his friends had bought
him new raiment and filled his purse in
Boston to attend the first Continental Congress. Governor Gage had just made his
proclamation offering pardon "to all persons who shall forthwith lay down their
Arms and return to the Duties of peaceable
Subjects, excepting only from the benefit of
such pardon Samuel Adams and John Hancock, whose Offences were of too flagitious a
Nature to admit of any other Consideration
than that of condign Punishment." The Battle
of Bunker Hill had been fought and Dr. Joseph
Warren had been killed. The letter was as
follows:

"My Dearest Betsy, yesterday I received
Letters from some of our Friends at the Camp
informing me of the Engagement between the
American troops and the Rebel Army at Char-
lestown. I cannot but be greatly rejoiced at
the tryed Valour of our Countrymen who

by all Accounts behaved with an intrepidity
becoming those who fought for their Liberties
against the mercenary Soldiers of a Tyrant.
It is painful to me to reflect on the Terror I
suppose you were under, on hearing the
Noise of War so near. Favour me, my
dear, with an Account of your Apprehen-
sions at that time, under your own hand.
I pray God to cover the heads of our Countrymen in every day of Battle and ever to
protect you from Injury in these distracted
times. The Death of our truly amiable and
worthy Friend Dr. Warren is greatly afflicting;
the language of Friendship is, how shall we
resign him; but it is our Duty to submit to the
Dispensations of Heaven 'whose ways are ever
gracious and just.' He fell in the glorious
Struggle for publick Liberty. Mr. Pitts and
Dr. Church inform me that my dear son has
at length escaped from the Prison at Boston. . . .
Remember me to my dear Hannah and sister
Polly and to all Friends. Let me know where
good old Surry is. Gage has made me respectable by naming me first among those who are
to receive no favour from him. I thoroughly
despise him and his proclamation. . . . The

Clock is now striking twelve. I therefore wish you good Night.

> "Yours most affectionately,
> "S. ADAMS."

Early in August, Samuel Adams and the other delegates from Massachusetts hurried home. Congress had adjourned from August 1st until September 5th, and when Adams arrived from Philadelphia, he found the "General Assembly of the Territory of Massachusetts Bay" in session and himself entitled to sit as one of the eighteen councillors. The delegation had in charge five hundred thousand dollars for the use of Washington's army. Samuel Adams was at once elected Secretary of State. Mrs. Adams, who had been forced to leave Boston, was living with her daughter at the home of her aged father in Cambridge, and Samuel Adams, Jr., held an appointment as surgeon in Washington's army. Friends were looking after all of them. Mr. Adams's visit with his family was a short one, and on September 12th, he started on his return to Philadelphia, travelling on horseback, on a horse loaned him by John Adams. An interesting letter is still preserved, written by

Mrs. Adams to her husband during this Congress. It is as follows:

CAMBRIDGE, Feb. 12, 1776.

MY DEAR—I received your affectionate Letter by Fesenton and I thank you for your kind Concern for my Health and Safty. I beg you Would not give yourself any pain on our being so Near the Camp; the place I am in is so Situated, that if the Regulars should ever take Prospect Hill, which God forbid, I should be able to make an Escape, as I am Within a few stones casts of a Back Road, Which Leads to the Most Retired part of Newtown. . . . I beg you to Excuse the very poor Writing as My paper is Bad and my pen made with Scissars. I should be glad (My dear), if you should n't come down soon, you would Write me Word Who to apply to for some Monney, for I am low in Cash and Every thing is very dear.

May I subscribe myself yours,

ELIZA^H ADAMS.

The closing years of Mrs. Adams's life brought more of peace and comfort than had been her portion during the Revolution or the years leading up to it from her marriage in 1764.

After the British evacuated Boston she and her family returned to the city to live. Sometimes they were "low in cash," as she naively put it, but with her fine sewing and Hannah's "exquisite embroidery," they managed to live in comfort. Samuel Adams retired from Congress in 1781, but was constantly in office in Massachusetts, the salary of which, while he did not much consider it, must have been of great help to her. During Hancock's incumbency of the gubernatorial chair Adams was Lieutenant-Governor, and upon the death of Hancock in 1793, Adams succeeded him as the chief executive of the State and was re-elected Governor in 1795 and '96, declining re-election because of failing health. The death of Dr. Samuel Adams in 1788, was a great blow to the father, which was somewhat ameliorated by his satisfaction at the happy marriage of his daughter Hannah, who had become the wife of Captain Thomas Wells, a younger brother of Mrs. Adams, her stepmother. They lived in a comfortable home on Winter Street. The last days of the aged pair were made comfortable by his son who, dying, left claims against the government which yielded about six thousand dollars. This sum

fortunately invested sufficed for the simple
wants of the old patriot and his wife. Samuel
Adams died in 1803 and his wife followed him
five years later.

Sarah Cobb Paine.

Sally Cobb Paine, wife of Robert Treat Paine,
one of the signers, was born and reared in Taunton,
Mass., where her father, Captain Thomas Cobb,
was a prominent citizen, magistrate, and member
of the legislature, who in 1754 had commanded
a Taunton company in the French and Indian
War. Her mother was Lydia Leonard, whose
father and grandfather, both, of whom were
called Captain James Leonard, had been prominent in the early history of Bristol County.
Her brother, Gen. David Cobb, served all
through the Revolution, three years of that
time being an aide on the staff of Washington.

Her early life and education did not differ
from that of other daughters of well-to-do and
church-going citizens of the commonwealth.
Robert Treat Paine, on his maternal side, a
grandson of Governor Robert Treat of Connecticut, was born in Boston. After graduating
from Harvard College, he studied for the ministry

but afterward changed his mind and read law
in the office of Benjamin Pratt, later Chief Justice
of the Colony of New York. After being admitted to the bar, Paine removed to Taunton
where he practised his profession for many
years. He was married to Sally Cobb about
1770. They had eight children, four sons and
four daughters. The oldest sons, Robert Treat,
Thomas, and Charles were educated for the law
and Henry the youngest for commercial business.
Robert Treat Paine, Jr., died of yellow fever in
1798, unmarried, and Thomas the second son,
by an act of the legislature, had his name
changed to Robert Treat Paine, Jr.

This young man brought great disappoint-
ment and unhappiness into the lives of his parents. Though educated for the law, he neglected
it and turned to writing in a desultory way. He
had marked ability but a temperament that
revolted from the strait-laced and somewhat
narrow life of a New England practitioner. In
February, 1795, he married Eliza Baker, daughter of an English actor and his wife, who were
touring the country. She seems to have been a
most worthy young woman, educated, refined,
and good principled, but at that time prejudice

against theatrical persons was very strong, especially among New England people, and the
elder Paine, on the day of his son's marriage,
drove him from his house. A friend of the
family, Major Wallach, gave shelter to the
young man and his wife and they remained
inmates of his family for fifteen months. It
is said that Mr. Paine offered "liberal remuner-
ation" but that his host would "only accept
one hundred dollars, and that reluctantly."
Robert Treat Paine, Jr., once remarked: "When
I lost a father I gained a wife and found a
friend."[8]   The brilliant but erratic young man
grew dissipated, lost, by some unfortunate
theatrical ventures, what money he had, and
finally, when broken in health and fortune and
dying of consumption, became reconciled to his
family and breathed his last in his father's home,
cared for by his mother and sister. It is need-
less to say that while he had been driven from his
father's house he had never gone out of his mother's heart. After the death of his son, which was
a greater blow to the father than most people
realised, he brought the young widow and the
three children of Robert Treat Paine, Jr., into
his own home, where they afterward lived.

Robert Treat Paine, Jr., wrote the famous political song *Adams and Liberty*, in 1798, when relations between the United States and both England and France were strained to the point of breaking and war, especially with France, seemed inevitable. The opening stanza of the song was as follows:

"Ye sons of Columbia, who bravely have fought
  For those rights which unstained from your sires have
     descended,
  May you long taste the blessings your valour has bought
  And your sons reap the soil which their fathers defended.
        'Mid the reign of mild peace,
        May your nation increase,
  With the glory of Rome and the wisdom of Greece;
  And ne'er shall the sons of Columbia be slaves,
  While the earth bears a plant or the sea rolls its waves."

Ann Thompson Gerry

Ann Thompson was a New York woman whom Elbridge Gerry, the young statesman from Massachusetts met and married during the time he was a member of the Continental Congress. She was the daughter of James Thompson and came from an old and highly honoured family. She was born in 1763 and educated in Dublin, Ireland, her two brothers being at the same time students of Edinburgh University, in Scotland.

They afterward entered the English army but never saw service in America.

Elbridge Gerry was in Congress almost continuously from 1776 until 1785, when he returned to private life, in Cambridge, Mass., introducing his young wife who became almost at once a social favourite. She was not long to enjoy the companionship of her husband, however, as, in 1797, Mr. Gerry was sent to France by President Adams and after his return from that mission was almost constantly in office, either in the service of the state or nation. Whatever his position was, however, whether member of Congress, Governor of his native State, or Vice-President of the United States, Mrs. Gerry proved herself a fitting helpmeet of her husband and cheerfully and gracefully met the demands of official and social life which devolved upon her. Her husband's biographer says of her, "She possessed considerable force of character and a dignified and gentle manner and, although an invalid, she personally superintended the education and religious training of her children and inspired them with a strong affection and reverence for herself which was evidenced by their devotion to her in her later years in New Haven."

In a letter to James Monroe on affairs of state, written by Mr. Gerry, in 1787, there appears this paragraph: "Your sentiments are perfectly correspondent with my own respecting domestic Happiness; it is the only Happiness in this life which in my opinion is worth pursuit. Our little pet is named Catharine after its Grand Mama, and is our Mutual delight."

Mr. Gerry died suddenly, in 1814, in the midst of his term of office as Vice-President. His biographer relates that shortly before he breathed his last "he drew from his bosom a miniature which he always wore when the original was absent. He spoke of it with an interest to show that although the surpassing beauty delineated in the picture might have first charmed the imagination, more enduring qualities had left the impress of affection on his heart."

Three sons and six daughters survived Mr. Gerry, as follows: Catharine, married to Hon. James T. Austin; Eliza, married to Major David Townsend; Ann, Elbridge, Thomas Russell, Helen Maria, Captain James Thompson, Eleanor Stanford, and Emily Louise, who died in New Haven, December 28, 1894, and was

the last surviving daughter of a signer of the
Declaration of Independence.[9]

Elbridge Gerry inherited a large fortune
from his father. After his death it was found
that the fortune had been to a great extent
sacrificed in the cause of his country, and Mrs.
Gerry disposed of the beautiful home in Cambridge and eventually settled in New Haven
where she died in 1849 and was buried in the
Old Cemetery, where sleep many of her children.
The inscription on her monument reads:

"Born Aug. 12, 1763; died March 17, 1849,
Ann, the widow of Elbridge Gerry, Vice-President of the U. S. His name is immortalised
on the Declaration of his country's Independence, hers in the transcendent virtues of domestic life. Both are embalmed in the veneration
of their children."

Sarah Scott Hopkins

Stephen Hopkins, alternately Governor and
Chief Justice of the Province of Rhode Island
for many years before his palsied hand wrote
its tremulous signature to the Declaration of
Independence, married Sarah Scott, daughter
of Silvanus and Joanna Jenckes Scott, as his

first wife, in 1726. Both were of Quaker stock
and both of them were barely turned twenty
years of age. Sarah Scott was a great-grand-
daughter of Richard Scott, said to be the first
Rhode Island man to embrace the Quaker faith.
Richard Scott's wife, Sarah Scott's great-grand-
mother, was Catharine Marbury, sister of Ann
Hutchinson, who was driven from Boston during the outbreak of religious intolerance that
characterised some of the earlier years of
the Massachusetts Bay Colony, and Catharine
Marbury, herself, was whipped in Boston gaol
for her religious contumacy. We know but
little of Sarah Scott Hopkins except that it is
recorded that she was "a kindly, industrious,
and frugal woman, a good mother and an
affectionate wife."

She was the mother of seven children, only
five of whom arrived at maturity. These
were as follows: Rufus, who married Abigail
Angell of Providence; John, who married Mary
Gibbs of Boston; Lydia, who became the second
wife of Col. Daniel Tillinghast of Newport; Silvanus, who died unmarried, and George, who
married Ruth Smith, daughter of his father's
second wife.

John Hopkins, the second son, died of small-
pox in 1753, off the coast of Spain. He was
master of the ship *Two Brothers* which at once
put into port, but the dead man, having been a
Protestant, was denied Christian burial. He
was twenty-four years old at the time of his
death.

Silvanus sailed the same year, 1753, for Cape
Breton, as mate of a small schooner, and on his
return was wrecked off the coast of Nova
Scotia. In attempting to return to Louisburg
in an open boat he was surprised by Indians on
the shore of St. Peter's Island and his body left
on the beach. Sarah Scott Hopkins died the
same year as her two sons, in the twenty-eighth
year of her married life.

Anne Smith Hopkins

Mrs. Anne Smith, the second wife of Stephen
Hopkins, was the daughter of Benjamin Smith,
of Providence, the same name as that borne by
her first husband though there was no relationship. She was a descendant, in the fourth
generation, from John Smith, one of the four
associates of Roger Williams, on his journey
from Massachusetts, in 1636.

Her marriage to Mr. Hopkins took place in 1755, in the Friends' Meeting-House in Smithfield, and the certificate, bearing the signatures of the bride, bridegroom, and witnesses, is still preserved in the collections of the Rhode Island Historical Society. She was thirty-eight years old at the time of her marriage, and brought with her three living children, Benjamin, Ruth, and Amery. It is said that Mr. Hopkins became very fond of his stepchildren as they did of him. Ruth Smith afterward married George Hopkins, the son of her stepfather, and Benjamin married Mary Tillinghast, a stepdaughter of Mr. Hopkins's daughter Lydia.

A few months after their marriage Mr. Hopkins was elected Governor of the Province and he continued in one office or another almost continuously until his death in 1785. His wife died two years before him.

Ann Remington Ellery

Ann Remington, daughter of Hon. Jonathan Remington of Cambridge, Mass., became in October, 1750, the first wife of William Ellery. She was a highly educated and accomplished young woman and a descendant from Governors

Dudley and Bradstreet, of the old Bay Colony.
William Ellery, son of well-to-do and well-
educated parents of Newport, R. I., was graduated from Harvard College in 1747, at the age
of twenty, and had just completed his legal
studies and begun the practice of law when he
retu..ned to Cambridge for his bride. She was
three years his junior and their new home in
Newport was a centre of refined and cultured
society. She died in 1764, after bearing him
seven children, four daughters and three sons.

Their oldest daughter, Elizabeth, born in 1751,
became the wife of Hon. Francis Dana, LL.D.,
member of Congress, Minister to Russia, and
Chief Justice of Massachusetts. Their son was
Richard H. Dana, the poet. A grandson of
the same name became a noted lawyer. Lucy
Ellery, the second daughter married William
Channing of Newport, Attorney - General of
Rhode Island, and their son was the eminent
divine William Ellery Channing. Almy, the
third daughter, became the wife of Hon. William
Stedman, who was a member of Congress from
1803 to 1810. William Ellery, Jr., the eldest son,
married Abigail, daughter of Captain William
Shaw and a noted beauty of her day. Edmund

Trowbridge Ellery, the younger son, was married to Catharine, daughter of Benjamin Almy.

Abigail Carey Ellery

William Ellery married Abigail, daughter of Nathaniel and Elizabeth Wanton Carey (or Cary), in 1767, three years after the death of his first wife. She was his second cousin and twenty-five years old at the time of their marriage., Mr. Ellery had prospered greatly in the practice of his profession and was accounted wealthy. He also stood high in the estimation of his townsmen and was keenly alive to their interests. From the beginning of the agitation against the encroachments of the British ministry, he had been outspoken in favour of the rights of the people. He was made to suffer greatly for this. His house was burned and his property greatly damaged at an early stage of the struggle but he did not give up his seat in Congress and return home as he would have been justified in doing; he left his own business affairs to get along as best they might while he continued service as one of the most indefatigable workers in Congress.

After the war, his own State made him Chief

Justice, and after the adoption of the Constitution
and the election of Washington to the Presidency
he was made collector of customs at Newport;
the competence he derived from these offices
proved sufficient to make his declining years
easy and comfortable.

Eight children were born to William Ellery
and his second wife, but only two of them lived
to grow to maturity.   One of these was George
Wanton Ellery, born in 1789, and for many
years collector of the port of Newport.   He
married Mary, daughter of Thomas Goddard,
and they lived in the old home of the signer.
The other child was a daughter, Mehitable
Redwood, who was born in 1784 and who married William Anthony.

Abigail Ellery died in 1793 and was survived
by her husband many years, he dying in 1820
in the ninety-third year of his age.

Elizabeth Hartwell Sherman

Elizabeth Hartwell, daughter of Deacon
Joseph Hartwell, of Stoughton, Mass., was
married to Roger Sherman, in 1749 and went
to live with him in New Milford, Conn., where
he held the office of County Surveyor for New

Haven County. Roger Sherman was twenty-eight years old at the time. Six years before he had removed from Stoughton to New Milford with his widowed mother and her little family, and worked at his calling as shoemaker. The young man was limited as to education, but he had ambition, a decided bent for mathematics, and great powers of application. In 1745, he began land surveying, and three years before his marriage we find him making the yearly calculations of an almanac that was published in New York. We know little about Elizabeth Hartwell Sherman beyond the fact that she became the mother of seven children and that she died in 1760, highly respected by all who knew her for her gentle nature and Christian character. At the time of her death, her husband was serving his fifth year as a member of Assembly, and was studying law. Their children were John, William, Isaac, Chloe, Oliver, Chloe, and Elizabeth. Chloe (the first), and Oliver died in infancy.

Rebecca Prescott Sherman

Rebecca Prescott Sherman, the gifted woman who became the second wife of Roger Sherman,

the patriot and signer of the Declaration of
Independence, was born in Salem, the first
child of Benjamin Prescott and Rebecca Minot
Prescott. Of her early life there is little to tell.
She came of a long line of distinguished men and
women and was a highly cultured and beautiful
girl of great spirit.

Her story is best told in the words of a gifted
descendant, Katharine Prescott Bennett, who
in a recent number of the *Journal of American
History*, quoting a niece of Rebecca
Prescott Sherman, writes: "She was born in
Salem, and nothing in particular happened to
her until she was about seventeen, when something *very particular indeed* happened. You
know that her aunt had married Rev. Josiah
Sherman of Woburn, Massachusetts, and one
bright morning, Aunt Rebecca started on horseback to visit her, little dreaming toward what
she was riding so serenely. Roger Sherman,
meanwhile, had just finished a visit to his
brother Josiah, who determined to ride a short
distance toward New Haven with him. They
were about to say good-bye when Aunt Rebecca's
horse, with its fair rider, came galloping down the
road. Aunt Rebecca was a great beauty and

a fine horsewoman, and she must have ridden straight into Roger Sherman's heart, for concluding to prolong his visit, he turned his horse and rode back with her. His courtship prospered, as we know, and they were married, May 12, 1763, when she was twenty and he was forty-two—twenty-two years her senior. She was his second wife and entered the life of this wonderfully gifted but plain man just at the time when her beauty, grace, and wit were of the greatest help in his career.

"We always have been a patriotic race, and this marriage brought Aunt Rebecca into still more active touch with all matters pertaining to the interests of the Colonies at this stirring period; and when at last the Declaration of Independence was promulgated, you can fancy the excitement and enthusiasm of the wife of Roger Sherman, the man who had so much to do with the momentous document. When, a little later, George Washington designed and ordered the new flag to be made by Betsy Ross, nothing would satisfy Aunt Rebecca but to go and see it in the works, and there she had the privilege of sewing some of the stars on the very first flag of a Young Nation. Perhaps because of this experience, she was chosen and requested to make the first flag ever made in the State of Connecticut—which she did, assisted by Mrs. Wooster. This fact is officially recorded."

The grey-haired and stately old lady, niece of Rebecca Prescott Sherman, being importuned for further reminiscences, continued: "A short story came to Uncle Roger's ears, which it amused him to tell, to Aunt Rebecca's consternation. When independence was declared, she was only thirty-four years old, and the lovely girl had developed into what George Washington considered the most beautiful of what we now call the Cabinet ladies. At a dinner given by General Washington to the political leaders and their wives, he took Aunt Rebecca out, thus making her the guest of honour. Madam Hancock was much piqued and afterward said to some one, that she was entitled to that distinction. A rumour of her displeasure came to the ear of George Washington, and to have his actions criticised was not at all to his liking. He drew himself up to his full height and sternly said: 'Whatever may be Mrs. Hancock's sentiments in the matter, I had the honour of escorting to dinner the handsomest lady in the room.' If Mrs. Hancock heard of this I do not think it would have tended to restore her tranquillity. I remember Aunt Rebecca coming into the room just as Uncle Roger was finishing this story and exclaiming half laughing, half vexed: 'Oh! Roger, why will you tell the child such nonsense?' Then turning to me, she said: 'Always remember, that handsome is as handsome does.' 'Well!' Uncle Roger retorted gallantly, 'you looked handsome and acted handsome too, Rebecca, so I am making an example of you. Surely you cannot find fault with that.' "

It was a saying of Roger Sherman that he never liked to decide a perplexing question without submitting it for the opinion of some intelligent woman, and as a usual thing, Mrs. Sherman was the woman whose opinion he desired. It is said that he consulted her not only in regard to his business affairs, which were of intimate concern to both of them, but in regard to public matters as well, and he placed great reliance on her judgment. For years Roger Sherman's connection with public affairs took him from home a great deal of his time, and to her fell the care of the family, not

only her own eight children but of his children
by his first wife.   That she met these responsibilities with ability and good judgment was at-
tested by the high position which the children
held.   It is also evident that although Rebecca
Sherman bore no part in the Revolution, she was
a worthy companion to the only man who signed
all four of the great state papers: The Address to
the King, the Declaration of Independence, the
Articles of Confederation, and the Constitution.

Rebecca Prescott Sherman became the mother
of eight children, all but one of whom arrived
at the age of maturity.   Their names were as
follows: Rebecca, Elizabeth, Roger, Mehitable,
Oliver, Martha, and Sarah.   Of these seven
children, one daughter became the mother of
United States Senator Hoar; another the mother
of Roger Sherman Baldwin, Governor of Connecticut and United States Senator; still another
the mother of the Honorable William M. Evarts.
These are but a few of the many eminent
descendants of this illustrious woman.[10]

Martha Devotion Huntington

Martha Devotion, eldest daughter of Rev.
Ebenezer Devotion and Martha Lathrop, was

married, in 1761, to Samuel Huntington of
Connecticut, who became signer of the Declaration of Independence, Governor of Connecticut,
and in 1779, President of the Continental Congress. She was twenty-two years old at the
time of her marriage, and her husband thirty,
and but recently established in the practice
of law. They lived in Norwich where Mr.
Huntington built up an extended practice and
began at an early day to take an active part in
political affairs of the Province. Politics was
no novelty to his wife, for the Rev. Ebenezer
Devotion, her father, was ardently interested
in the politics of Connecticut and represented
Windham in the General Assembly, from 1760
until 1771, the year of his death.

No children were born to Martha Huntington
and her husband but they adopted two children
of his brother, Rev. Joseph Huntington, who
were carefully reared and educated. One of
these children, Samuel Huntington, became
Governor of Ohio, in 1810 and 1811. The
other child, Frances, became the wife of Rev.
Edward Door Griffin, at one time President of
Williams College.

Martha Huntington died in 1794, in her

fifty-sixth year and her distinguished husband, two years later, aged sixty-five. Their remains rest side by side in the old burying ground at Norwich.

Mary Trumbull Williams

Mary Trumbull, second daughter of "Brother Jonathan" Trumbull, War Governor of Connecticut, was married, in 1771, to William Williams, one of the most prominent citizens of Lebanon, which town he had represented for many years in the General Assembly. She was twenty-five years old at the time of her marriage and was a handsome, educated, and accomplished young woman of excellent family.

It seems to have been a most advantageous mating. Mr. Williams was a successful and prosperous business man and also held the office of Town Clerk as well as Member of Assembly. He took his bride to a handsome home, not far from the big house of his father-in-law, which was to be known during the Revolution as the "War Office." Jonathan Trumbull was the only Colonial governor to remain true to the cause of the Colonies, and patriots from all parts of New

England came to consult with him and lay plans for future action.

To few women of the Revolutionary period was it given to stand in such close relation with the great men who were supporting the cause. Her public-spirited husband, who had for years watched the gradual encroachment on the rights of the Colonies by the British ministry and who, through his association with British officers during the time he served in the French and Indian War, had come to know the contempt in which they held the Colonies and their rights. Moreover, he was the trusted son-in-law of Governor Trumbull who was in constant correspondence with Samuel Adams and the other patriots of Massachusetts, and the confidant and adviser of General Washington. More than most women of her time, Mary Trumbull understood the condition of affairs during the years leading up to the Declaration of Independence, and we may be sure that it was a proud day for her when her husband was elected a delegate to Congress in 1775.

He was then colonel of the Twelfth Regiment of militia. He promptly resigned as he could not possibly attend to the duties of both posi-

tions. He seems also to have realised that it
was no holiday occasion that he was entering
upon; he closed out all his business leaving
himself entirely foot free to attend to public
affairs. And in all these actions we are told, he
was loyally upheld and supported by his wife
whose patriotism and public spirit were equal
to his own. Throughout the entire war their
home was thrown open to soldiers, and during
the winter of 1781 they gave up their own house
to the officers of a detachment of soldiers
stationed near them, and took other quarters
for themselves.

The following anecdote is related: At a meeting of the Council of Safety in Lebanon, near the
close of 1776, when the prospects of our success
looked dark, two members of the Council were
invited to the home of Mr. and Mrs. Williams,
Benjamin Huntington and William Hillhouse.
The conversation turned upon the gloomy out-
look. Mr. Hillhouse expressed hope and confidence. "If we fail," said Mr. Williams, "I know
what my fate will be. I have done much to prose-
cute the war; and one thing I have done which the
British will never pardon—I have signed the
Declaration of Independence; I shall be hanged."

"Well," said Mr. Huntington, "if we fail I shall be exempt from the gallows, for my name is not attached to the Declaration, nor have I ever written anything against the British Government."

"Then, sir," said Colonel Williams turning upon him, "you deserve to be hanged for not doing your duty."

Three children were born to Mary Williams and her husband: Solomon, who was born January 6, 1772, and who died in 1810, in New York; Faith, born September 29, 1774, who married John McClellan of Woodstock; and William T., born March 2, 1779, and who married his cousin, Sarah Trumbull.

The death of Solomon Williams was a great blow to his father who died within a year, his last words being the name of his son. Mrs. Williams survived her husband nearly twenty years, dying at Lebanon in 1831.

Laura Collins Wolcott

Laura Collins, who was married to Oliver Wolcott, in January, 1759, was the daughter of Captain Daniel and Lois Cornwall Collins of Guilford, Connecticut. She was a fine type of New England girl, descended from the first settlers, and brought up in the manner of Connecticut girls of well-to-do families of that day. The *National Cyclopædia of American Biography* says of her: "She was a woman of almost masculine strength of mind, energetic and thrifty; and while Governor Wolcott was away from home, attended to the management of their farm, educated their younger children, and made it possible for her husband to devote his energies to his country."

Her husband was the youngest son of Roger Wolcott, a former governor of the State and was thirty-three years old at the time of their marriage, ten years the senior of the bride he brought to his home in the old town of Litchfield. He had graduated from Yale College, and had served as captain of a company of his own raising in the wars along the northern frontiers, under a commission from Governor George Clinton of New York. He studied medicine under Dr. Alexander Wolcott of Windsor. He had never practised, however, as the General Assembly created the new county of Litchfield in 1771, and appointed him sheriff. This office he still held at the time of his marriage. It was fortu-

nate for the material interests of Oliver Wolcott
that his young wife was "of almost masculine
strength of mind, energetic and thrifty," as he
had so many public matters to look after that
his own affairs must have suffered. He continued in the militia, rising rank by rank until he
was major-general. In 1774 he was elected to
the council and continued a member until his
election as Lieutenant-Governor in 1786. A
large part of the time that he was a member
of the Continental Congress he was also in the
field with the army or engaged in recruiting and
organising troops for the army. In 1796, he
was elected Governor and continued in that
office until his death. During many of these
years, almost the entire burden of directing
his domestic affairs rested on the shoulders
of his wife. Extracts from the letters, which
he wrote to her during his absence, throw an
interesting light upon the characters of both
Laura Wolcott and her husband —rather upon hers by inference, as her letters to him
are not preserved while the letters he wrote
to her are most of them in possession of the
descendants. From Philadelphia in 1776, he
wrote:

"My Dear—I feel much concerned for the Burden which necessarily devolves upon you. I hope you will make it as light as possible. . . . You may easily believe that the situation of publick Affairs is such that the critical Moment is near which will perhaps decide the Fate of the Country; and that the business of Congress is very interesting. Yet if any excuse can reasonably be allowed for my returning, I shall think myself justified in doing so. The circumstances of my affairs demand it."

In a letter written from Philadelphia, January 21, 1777, he says: ". . . I am not able to give you the least Advice in the Conduct of my Business. Your own Prudence in the direction of it I have no doubt of. I only wish that the Cares which oppress you were less. . . . I fear that by Reason of the scarcity of many articles in Connecticut, you find a Difficulty in supplying the Family with some Things that may be wanted. But I trust the Essentials of Life you are provided with and I wish that you may not want any of its conveniences. . . ."

Mr. Wolcott wrote in March, 1777: "I have this instant rec'd a Letter from Dr. Smith, of the

12th, wherein he tells me that you and the children have been inoculated for the Small Pox and that he apprehended you were so far thro' it as to be out of Danger, Casualities excepted. . . . I perceive that Mariana has had it bad—he wrote, very hard. I am heartily sorry for what the little Child has suffered, and very much want to see her. If she has by this lost some of her Beauty, which I hope she has not, yet I well know she might spare much of it and still retain as much as most of her sex possesses."

The patriotism of Laura Wolcott was in keeping with that of her husband. Her home was thrown open at all times to those who were in any way aiding the cause. And while Oliver Wolcott gave freely of his money for patriotic purposes, she furnished blankets, stockings, and supplies from their farm for the army, almost continuously. Laura Wolcott did not live to see her husband in the governor's chair, passing away in April, 1794, in the fifty-eighth year of her age. Governor Wolcott died in 1797, aged seventy-one years.

Five children were born to Laura Wolcott and her husband, three sons and two daughters; one

son died in infancy; the other children were as
follows: Oliver, born 1760, married Elizabeth
Stoughton; Laura, born 1761, married William
Moseley; Mary Ann (or Mariana), born 1765,
married Chauncey Goodrich, and Frederick,
born 1767, married Betsey Huntington first and,
afterward, Sally Worthington Cooke."

"Among the families, not native or to the
manner born, that shed lustre on the social life
of New York while the Republican court was
held there none were more illustrous, by heredi-
tary worth and personal excellence, than those of
the Wolcotts of Connecticut," says a well-known
writer of the early years of the last century.
"The name of Wolcott had been identified, for
more than a century and a half, with the management of Colonial affairs in New England.
Oliver Wolcott had been Governor of Connecticut
and was a signer of the Declaration of Independence. His son and namesake, when about thirty
years of age, was appointed auditor of the treasury, and his memoirs are overflowing with interesting acts and discussions, political and social,
at a time when republicanism was crystallising
from mere enthusiasm and theory into a national
habit and life. Young Oliver Wolcott had grad-

Mrs. Chauncey Goodrich.
(Mary Ann Wolcott.)
From an engraving by J. Rogers.

uated at Yale College with Joel Barlow, Zephaniah
Swift, and Noah Webster, and after his admission
to the Hartford bar, he had been of the famous
company of 'Connecticut wits,' including Trum-
bull, the author of *MacFingal*, Dr. Lemuel Hop-
kins author of *The Hypocrite's Hope*, Richard
Alsop, one of the authors of the *Echo* and the
Political Greenhouse, Joel Barlow, known for his
Vision of Columbus, Noah Webster, Theodore
Dwight, and others.

"When Oliver Wolcott came to New York to
live, he speedily became noted for his wit and
conversational brilliancy and was eagerly sought
for as a guest. Perhaps no more interesting and
valuable guide to the inner life of the time could
be found than the memoirs he left behind him.
When several years later, Alexander Hamilton
resigned the Treasury Department young Oliver
Wolcott was selected as his successor. Wolcott
was no less known for the transparent simplicity
and integrity of his character than for his intellectual powers and unremitting devotion to the
public duty. His wife, though not one of the
recognised beauties of the time, had a counte-
nance of much loveliness and a very graceful
manner. It was said that there were few ladies

of the time who could compare with her in refined cultivation and intelligence.

"Mary Ann, daughter of the signer, who spent much of her time in New York with her brother's family and afterward in Philadelphia, was one of the most beautiful women of her age. Wherever she moved in society, she was the centre of an admiring crowd, and she heightened and confirmed, by the vivacity of her wit, which she shared in common with her family, the impression made by her personal charms. This lady, after breaking many of the bachelor hearts of New York and Philadelphia, was married to Chauncey Goodrich whose abilities and character were worthy of the choice she made."

Hannah Jones Floyd

Hannah Jones,[12] daughter of William Jones of Southampton, L. I., was married to William Floyd of Setauket, L. I., in 1760 (or '61). He was a wealthy young farmer who had received a liberal education but chose to superintend the estate left him by his father, rather than enter upon a professional or business career. But little is known of the young woman beyond the fact that she was a capable, well-brought-up girl, who, from the time her husband began to take part in public life, which was as delegate to the first Continental Congress which convened in Philadelphia in 1774, was left with the practical management of his affairs. William Floyd was already in command of the militia of Suffolk County and active in county and local matters. He was re-elected to the Congress of 1775 and 1776, and was one of the first of the signers to suffer personally for the stand which he had taken.

General Floyd's estate included a fine plantation, highly productive and well stocked, and with an abundance of fruit and ornamental trees, many acres of fine timber and firewood, and a handsome mansion. Lying contiguous to New York with its ready market, it was highly valuable. As soon as the American troops were withdrawn from Long Island, the British took possession of the farm. Mrs. Floyd and her little family were forced to fly across into Connecticut for safety and for seven years the family derived no benefit from their property. Every bit of the live stock and the crops that had been planted were taken by the British, the barns, and even the house, were used for the stabling of the horses of the British troops, the fruit and ornamental trees were wantonly cut down, and acres of the timber destroyed and such serious inroads made upon his patrimony that after the establishment of peace, General Floyd declined further re-election to Congress or to the State Senate where he had done eminent service, and retired to begin life anew at the age of sixty-nine years, to an unbroken tract of land which he had purchased on the Mohawk River.

His wife did not live to take part in this migration; the anxieties and hardships to which she had been subjected had undermined her health and she passed away, May 16, 1781, in the forty-first year of her age. She was a public-spirited and patriotic woman and upheld uncomplainingly the course her husband pursued, and all his public actions.

Hannah Floyd was the mother of three children, one son and two daughters. Nicoll Floyd, the oldest of the children, married Phebe Gelston, daughter of David Gelston of New York. Mary Floyd, the eldest daughter, married Col. Benjamin Tallmadge of Litchfield, Conn., and Catharine, the second, married Dr. Samuel Clarkson of Philadelphia.

In 1783, General Floyd married as his second wife Joanna Strong of Setauket, L. I., by whom he had two children, Ann, who married, first George W. Clinton, son of the Vice-President, and second, Abraham Varick of New York. Eliza, the youngest married James Platt of Utica.

Christina Ten Broeck Livingston

Christina Ten Broeck, the wife of Philip Livingston, fourth son of the second Lord of the Livingston Manor, and distinguished as "Philip the Signer," came of that sturdy, thrifty Dutch stock that for the first century, after the founding of New Amsterdam, dominated the sparse Colony that was being built up along the Hudson River. Her great grandfather, Dirck Wesselse Ten Broeck, was an Indian trader, and the first record we have of him is when, in 1663, he bought from her heirs, the house and lot in Beverwyck, formerly owned and occupied by Annetje Jans Bogardus, paying for the property 1000 guilders in beaver skins. When the "ancient town of Beverwyck or Albany" received its charter in 1686, Dirck Wesselse Ten Broeck was named first in the list of alderman. Afterward, he was

Recorder and then Mayor. His son was also
Alderman and Recorder and his grandson
Richard (or Dirck) who married Margarita
Cuyler, was also a man of affairs, Alderman,
Recorder, and Mayor. Christina was their
third child.

Philip and Christina Livingston were married
about 1740. He was a prosperous young business man in New York and soon began to take
an interest in public affairs, being elected Alderman from the East Ward in 1754 and re-elected
for nine years in succession. He was a member
of the Provincial Assembly together with George
Clinton, Pierre Van Cortlandt, General Philip
Schuyler, Abraham Ten Broeck, and Charles
DeWitt. He was chosen a member of the first
Congress that met in Philadelphia in 1774, during
which session John Adams wrote of him in his
diary: "Philip Livingston is a great, rough,
rapid mortal. There is no holding any conversation with him. He blusters away—says if England should turn us adrift, we should instantly
go to civil wars among ourselves, to determine
which Colony should govern all the rest." Either
Philip Livingston changed his mind or else had
intentionally misled the young Bostonian, for in

the next Congress his name was placed on the Declaration of Independence.

At this time, Mrs. Livingston and her younger children were living on Brooklyn Heights and it was in his house that the council of war was held at which the American generals decided upon the retreat from Long Island. Philip Livingston, himself, was at the time in Philadelphia in attendance upon Congress. Soon afterward the family removed to Esopus (Kingston, N. Y.).

In 1778, at the most gloomy period of the Revolution, Mr. Livingston, broken in health, tried to rest from his public duties and visit his family but at the urgent request of the state government returned to Congress. He felt that he would never come back home, and bid his friends in Kingston and Albany good-bye. This was in March and in June following he died, with no member of his family with him except his son Henry who was serving as aide on General Washington's staff. Henry learned of his father's condition and hurried to his side and remained until the old patriot breathed his last on June 12th.

Nine children were born to Christina and Philip Livingston, as follows: Philip Philip, born

in Albany in 1741, settled in Jamaica, W. I.,
where he married Sarah Johnson of the Parish of
St. Andrews, in June, 1768. He left a number
of children, most of whom returned to the United
States and became citizens. He is said to have
been the only one of the signer's children to leave
children. The second son, Richard, died unmarried. Catharine, the third child, married, first,
Stephen Van Rensselaer and second Rev. Eilar-
dus Westerlo of Albany. Margaret, the fourth
child, married Dr. Thomas Jones of New York.
The fifth child, Peter Van Brugh, died, unmarried, of yellow fever in Jamaica, W. I. Sarah,
the sixth, was married to her cousin, Dr. John H.
Livingston, who became President of Queen's
College (now Rutger's), New Brunswick, N. J.
The seventh child was Henry Philip, who became
an officer in Washington's Life Guard. Abraham,
the eighth child, was Commissary of Provisions
to the Continental Army in 1776. While in the
service in the south he was captured by the
British and sent to prison in Charleston. He
seems to have died there unmarried, prior to
1782. Alida, the ninth child, died unmarried.

Edward Livingston, son of Philip Philip, was
born in Jamaica and brought to this country in

1784 at the age of four or five years. In 1830 he was elected Lieutenant-Governor of New York. He married a daughter of Chancellor Livingston and lived at Clermont on the Hudson.

Elizabeth Annesley Lewis

Elizabeth Annesley Lewis, wife of Francis Lewis, was, like Hannah Floyd, driven to an untimely death by the hardships and persecutions she was forced to undergo from the British, because her husband was a signer of the Declaration of Independence. Not much of definite information has come down to us of her girlhood or antecedents but what we have is evidence of her high character and undaunted spirit.

The story of the early life of Francis Lewis reads like a romance. The orphaned son of a Welsh clergyman of the Church of England, he received a classical education, supplemented by two years' training in the counting-room of a great mercantile house in London. Then, upon attaining his majority he found himself possessed of a considerable sum of money, which he invested in a stock of merchandise that he brought to New York. As the city was comparatively small, his consignment of goods was in

danger of overstocking the market. In consequence, he formed a partnership with Edward
Annesley, a prominent young merchant, and
leaving a portion of the cargo with him to dispose
of, he carried the remainder to Philadelphia, and
made a large profit. He returned to New York
to take up a permanent residence, and married
his partner's younger sister, Elizabeth. He entered extensively into foreign commerce. In
the prosecution of his business, he travelled
widely in Europe. Twice he visited Russia,
pushing his trade into all the sea-ports from St.
Petersburg to Archangel. He visited the islands
of Northern Scotland and suffered shipwreck on
the coast of Ireland. He took an active part in
the French War and was with his friend Col.
Mersey (or Mercer) in the fort of Oswego, as a
purchaser of supplies for the British troops,
when Montcalm reduced the fort and captured
the garrison. Col. Mersey was killed and Lewis,
who was acting as his aide, was made prisoner,
and taken to Canada and afterward sent to
France where he was exchanged. At the close
of the war, the British Government gave him
for his services 5000 acres of land.

About 1765, Lewis moved his family to Whitestone, L. I., where he acquired a handsome estate. He retired from business but returned to New York in 1771 for the purpose of establishing his son, Francis Lewis, Jr., in business. He removed his family back to Long Island again in 1775 and there Mrs. Lewis resided permanently, though her husband and sons were away a large portion of the time. Francis Lewis devoted his attention entirely to public affairs after his election to the first Continental Congress.

Like Floyd, Livingston, and Robert Morris, the other New York signers, Francis Lewis was proscribed by the British authorities and a price set upon his head. The enemy did not stop there. Very soon after they were in possession of Long Island, Captain Birtch was sent with a troop of light horse "to seize the lady and destroy the property." As the soldiers advanced on one side, a ship of war from the other fired upon the house. There was nothing to be done. Mrs. Lewis looked calmly on. A shot from the vessel struck the board on which she stood. One of her servants cried: "Run, Mistress, run." She replied: "Another shot is not likely to strike the same spot," and did not change her place. The soldiers entered the house and began their work of plunder and devastation. One of them threw himself at her feet and tore the buckles from her shoes. The buckles looked like gold but were nothing but pinchbeck. "All is not gold that glitters," she remarked to the discomfited young man. The soldiers destroyed books, papers, and pictures, ruthlessly broke up furniture, and then, after pillaging the house, departed taking Mrs. Lewis with them. She was carried to New York and thrown into prison. She was not allowed a bed or a change of clothing and only the coarse and scanty food that was doled out each day to the other prisoners. For three weeks this continued during which time she was not permitted to communicate with any one outside. Then a negro man, an old family servant, who had followed her to the city, managed to find out where she was and to smuggle some small articles of clothing and some food in to her, and also to carry letters which he contrived to send through the lines to her friends. The matter was taken up by Congress and referred to the Board of War and demands made upon the British for her better treatment. The British were bent on making an example of her because of her wealth and prominence, and the poor woman found little relief. Finally, after nearly three months, the matter was brought to the attention of General Washington, who ordered the arrest of Mrs. Barren, wife of the British Paymaster-General and Mrs. Kempe, wife of the Attorney-General of Pennsylvania, at their homes in Philadelphia. They were confined to their own homes, under guards, and the intimation carried to the British authorities that unless an exchange was arranged immediately they would be subjected to the same treatment as was being received by Mrs. Lewis. The exchange was made, but Mrs. Lewis was not permitted to leave New York City.

Hardly had she a roof over her head than she was called upon to face a new trouble. The aged coloured man-servant who had followed and served her and remained in the city, doing what little he could toward ameliorating her condition, was sick—almost at death's door. He was a Roman Catholic in religion and would not die without the last rites of his church. There was not a priest in New York and it seemed impossible to get one as the city was under martial law. Mrs. Lewis, weak and suffering from her long

imprisonment and scarcely possessing the necessaries of life, yet contrived to send a messenger
to Philadelphia, who found a priest there and
helped smuggle him through the British lines
into New York, in time to administer to the
dying man who passed away in peace.

Mrs. Lewis never recovered from the inhuman
treatment she had received at the hands of the
British.   After some months she was allowed
to join her husband in Philadelphia.   It was
plain to be seen, however, that she was broken in
health and constitution and was slowly sinking
into the grave.   Early in 1779, Francis Lewis,
now elected for the fourth time a member of the
Continental Congress, asked leave of absence in
order to devote his whole time to his wife.   About
the same time, her second son, Col. Morgan
Lewis, married Gertrude, daughter of Robert
Livingston of Clermont and took his bride to
Philadelphia to introduce her to his mother.   A
few days later, she sank to her rest.

Three children were born to Elizabeth Lewis
and her husband: Francis, the eldest son, was
married to the daughter of a Tory named Lud-
low, whose family strenuously objected to the
young man, "because his father would certainly

be hung." Col. Morgan Lewis, the second son, married Gertrude, the daughter of Robert Livingston and Margaret Beekman, his wife. She was a sister of Chancellor Livingston and of Edward, "The Jurist." Ann Lewis, the only daughter of Elizabeth and Francis Lewis, fell in love with a post-captain in the British navy, named Robertson. Her father refused to consent to their marriage and a clandestine wedding ensued. Had she remained in America, it is probable that a reconciliation would have been effected, but as Captain Robertson and his bride soon after sailed for England all intercourse ceased. Robertson was a brave, reckless sort of man, it is said, not given to taking much thought of the morrow. When in years afterward Mrs. Robertson was left a widow in straitened circumstances a small sum of money was sent her every year anonymously and it was not until the death of Queen Charlotte, wife of George III, that the identity of the donor was made known. The Queen was reported to have said that the wife of a gallant sailor like Captain Robertson ought not to suffer penury. One of Mrs. Robertson's daughters married Sumner, Archbishop of Canterbury, another married Wilson, Archbishop of

Calcutta, and a third became the wife of Sir James Moncrief, Lord Advocate of Scotland.

"In the war of the Revolution," writes Julia Delafield, a granddaughter of the signer, in her biography of Francis Lewis, "Mrs. Lewis had more than one opportunity of showing the steady purpose, the firmness of nerve that would have distinguished her had she been a man. . . . To Francis Lewis she was Heaven's best gift. When his adventurous spirit led him to embark on long and perilous voyages, he knew that he left his children to the care of an able as well as a tender mother, who could train their characters as well as protect their interests. The conduct and careers of her children is the best eulogy of Mrs. Francis Lewis."

Mary Walton Morris

Mary Walton, who became the wife of Lewis Morris in 1749, came of a notable family of New York merchants. Her father was Jacob Walton who had married Maria, daughter of Dr. Gerardus Beekman, and with his brother William carried on the great business founded by their father.

"But the most historic family of merchants

was that of Walton, whose wealth was cited in parliament to show the wealth of the Province," says James Grant Wilson's *History of New York City.* "The founder of the family was William Walton, a patronymic which was also carried through the full century. Early in the eighteenth century he purchased ground on the East River water front, and there established extensive shipyards. . . . He sailed his own vessels to the West Indies and the Spanish Main. The origin of the great fortune of this enterprising family was an extensive preference granted to Captain Walton (or Boss Walton, as he was familiarly called on account of his superintending work in the shipyard) by the Spaniards of St. Augustine, Fla., and the West India Islands. He had the contract to supply the garrison and had a permanent factor at the Florida post. His son was William Walton who sailed his father's ships." After the death of the founder, the business was carried on under the firm name of Jacob and William Walton and after the death of Jacob, by William Walton and Jacob Walton's children.

Mary Walton was an eminently capable woman and notwithstanding her wealth and social position .was a well-trained and thrifty housewife and entered actively into the rural life that her husband had chosen for himself when he graduated from Yale College in 1746 and as the elder son, succeeded to the proprietorship of the manorial estate of Morrisania intending to devote himself to agricultural pursuits.

Ten children were born to them as follows: Lewis, Jacob, William, James Staats, Richard V., Catharine, Mary, Sarah, and Helena. The three oldest sons all entered the army and acquitted themselves with great credit.

Notwithstanding his large property lying close to New York City and almost certain to suffer, Lewis Morris was in advance of most public men of New York in counselling resistance to British encroachment upon the rights of the people and naturally was a marked man when he signed the Declaration. His family were forced to fly for safety and his magnificent estate was almost entirely despoiled. His house was ruined and his farm wasted. His cattle were driven off and appropriated to the subsistence of the invader. His beautiful forest of more than a thousand acres was given up to havoc and spoil. As illustrative of the disorganised condition of affairs in the Morris household at this time and also as showing how much Mr. Morris was obliged to rely on his wife and how capable she was to act, is shown in the following letters written to him by his son Lewis, who was stationed in New York:

NEW YORK, Sept. 6th, 1776.

Dr. SIR,—

When I received your letter I was at the Bridge looking for a Sloop to carry some Furniture to the Fish Kill, which I shall send off next day after to Morrow. From your Letter I believe you were acquainted with Mama's moving up to Harrison's Purchase with her Family where she carried a great deal of Furniture and all her Linnen and wearing apparel, therefore your Proposition of moving her to Philadelphia will be attended by many obstacles, for she can neither bring Cloathes sufficient for the Family nor Utensils to keep house; as most of the Carts and Waggons are pressed in the service. . . . I assure you, Sir, your affairs at Morrisania however secure you may think they may be are in a very critical situation, in all probability they may be in the Possession of the Enemy in a little Time. . . . I wish you was at home to assist me, you have a good deal at stake. . . . Mrs. Wilkins has very industriously propagated that you had fled to France. Such Brimstones will certainly meet with their desert.

Give my love to all, and believe me to be, Your dutiful son,

L. MORRIS.

On September 14th, a week after the letter above was written, the young man writes again to his father:

"Dr. PAPA, . . . I have compleated a Task the most difficult that ever poor Lad undertook; but I am sure you will think it very imperfectly compleated. The danger of our Situation required Dispatch—Dispatch created confusion which caused a Deficiency in Many Parts of my system. However I so far settled the plan of my Mother's Removel, that I believe she left her dreary habitation last Thursday attended by a very large Retinue—The Chariot before the chair, and three horses in the centre and the Waggon brought up the rear. I hope they may arrive safe. . . . The Enemy has possession of Montroseur's Island for these three or four days and yesterday they brought several Field Pieces upon the North West Point and fired several times at your house. I suppose they will shoot it like a sieve and destroy what little I left on the place. . . ."

Mr. Morris left Congress in 1777, being succeeded by his brother, Gouverneur. He continued his service, however, part of the time as a member of the state legislature and a part of the time in the field with the state militia. At the close of the war after the evacuation of New York by the British he returned to Morrisania with his family and cheerfully began the work of bringing back the nearly ruined estate to the semblance of a home. The remains of Mary Walton Morris and her distinguished husband rest in the family vault at St. Ann's Church (Episcopal), St. Ann's Avenue and 40th Street, Bronx, New York.

Jacob Morris, the second son of the signer, who entered the Revolution at the age of nineteen became a general and at the close of the war retired to the "Morris Patent," a three-thousand acre tract of wild land granted to his uncle, Col. Richard Morris, and his father, in Montgomery

County. He married Mary Cox, an amiable, high-spirited girl who bravely took up the pioneer life with him and went into the wilderness to break ground and build up a home. Her mother-in-law, Mary Walton, must have appreciated her endeavours and the contrasts of her life, for though perhaps as was the custom of the day she indulged little in correspondence she summed up her courage and indicted an epistle to her son Jacob, saying, "I am glad Polly is learning how to spin and that she is taking an interest in the chickens."

Annis Boudinot Stockton

Annis Boudinot, who became the wife of Richard Stockton, one of the most prominent young lawyers of New Jersey in 1762, was a woman of far more than ordinary intellectual ability and of a high character and patriotic spirit that made her a fitting companion for the man whose devotion to the cause of independence brought him to his death before his time.

She was of French Huguenot descent, her family having come to America soon after the Revocation of the Edict of Nantes in 1686. Her father, Elias Boudinot, was for a time a silversmith in Princeton and her brother, who bore the same name as their father, studied law in the office of Richard Stockton and married his sister, Hannah Stockton.

Richard Stockton was highly successful in the practice of his profession and had added materially to the large estate he inherited from his father, when he married Annis Boudinot and took her to "Morven," his handsome Colonial home, near Princeton. "Morven" was known for its hospitality and as a gathering place for some of the brightest minds of the day. They were living here, when Mr. Stockton was elected a delegate to the Continental Congress, and it was here that she performed a service which was made historic. When the British under Cornwallis came to Princeton in 1776, Mrs. Stockton secured and secreted a number of important state papers as well as the rolls and records of the American Whig Society of Princeton College, an act for which her name was added as an honorary member of the Society. Congress was then sitting in Baltimore and Mr. Stockton hastened home to conduct his family to a place of safety. He hurried them out of Princeton to Monmouth County, about thirty

miles away, and then returning, went to spend
the night with a friend, a patriot named Cowen-
hoven. That night a party of Tories came and
arrested the two men. They were dragged from
their bed at a late hour and half clad carried
away and thrown into prison. Mr. Stockton
was first taken to Amboy where he was confined
in the common gaol, suffering greatly from the
cold. From there he was carried to the prison
in New York, where he was most inhumanly
treated. All the comforts and many of the
necessities of life were withheld from him, notwithstanding the delicate condition of his health,
and his high and honourable standing as a man.
At one time he was left for twenty-four hours
without food and then supplied only with the
coarsest and not enough of that. Through the
efforts of Mrs. Stockton, Congress was informed
of these facts, and General Howe was given to
understand that unless Mr. Stockton received
better treatment in the future, retaliation would
be taken on British prisoners. His condition
was somewhat improved after that, but it was
too late. The seeds had been sown of the disease that was eventually to carry him to his
grave. The British plundered his beautiful home,

burned his splendid library and papers, and drove off his stock, much of which was blooded and highly valuable. The devastation of his estate, especially all that portion that could in any way be productive, taken together with the depreciation in value of the Continental currency, so embarrassed Mr. Stockton financially that he was obliged to apply to friends for temporary assistance in order to supply his family with the necessaries of life. This caused a depression of spirits from which he never rallied and hastened the ravages of the disease that brought him to an untimely death in 1781, in the fifty-first year of his age.

Mrs. Stockton, who was three years younger than her husband, continued to live at "Morven" until her son Richard was married, when she relinquished her home to him and took up her residence in a house at the corner of Washington and Nassau streets, Princeton. Her youngest daughter, Abigail, lived with her until her own marriage to Robert Field of Whitehill, Burlington County, a brother of the wife of her brother Richard.

Richard Stockton left two sons and four daughters. Richard, the eldest son, born April 17, 1764, became one of the most eminent lawyers

of the day. He left a number of children of
whom the late Robert F. Stockton was one.
The other son was Lucius Horatio, who also
became a prominent lawyer and was appointed
Secretary of War in 1801, by President Adams.

Richard Stockton's eldest daughter, Julia, married Dr. Benjamin Rush of Philadelphia, also a
signer of the Declaration of Independence. Susan
Stockton, the second daughter married Alexander
Cutbert of Canada. Mary married Rev. Andrew
Hunter, D.D., who was a chaplain in the Continental Army and a professor in Princeton.

Annis Boudinot was well known throughout
the Revolution for her patriotic verse. One of
her poems drew a courtly acknowledgment from
General Washington to whom it was addressed.
Another, *Welcome, Mighty Chief, Once More!* was
sung by the young women of Trenton while
Washington was passing through Princeton on
his way to his first inauguration.

Mrs. Stockton wrote the following upon the
announcement of peace in 1783:

"With all thy country's blessings on thy head,
   And all the glory that encircles man,
Thy deathless fame to distant nations spread,
   And realms unblest by Freedom's genial plan;

Addressed by statesmen, legislators, kings,
  Revered by thousands as you pass along,
While every muse with ardour spreads her wings
  To our hero in immortal song;
Say, can a woman's voice an audience gain;
  And stop a moment thy triumphal car?
And wilt thou listen to a peaceful strain,
  Unskilled to paint the horrid wrack of war?
For what is glory—what are martial deeds—
  Unpurified at Virtue's awful shrine?
Full oft remorse a glorious day succeeds,
  The motive only stamps the deed divine.
But thy last legacy, renowned chief,
  Hath decked thy brow with honours more sublime,
Twined in thy wreath the Christian's firm belief,
  And nobly owned thy faith to future time."

Washington sent an answer to this ode and the letter which she wrote enclosing it. Her letter is lost, but we have the ode given above and his reply which is as follows:

ROCKY HILL, Sept. 24th, 1783.

You apply to me, my dear madam, for absolution, as though you had committed a crime, great in itself yet of the venial class. You have reasoned good, for I find myself strongly disposed to be a very indulgent ghostly adviser on this occasion, and notwithstanding you are the most offending soul alive (that is if it is a crime to write elegant poetry), yet if you will come and

dine with me on Thursday, and go through the
proper course of penitence which shall be pre-
scribed, I will strive hard to assist you in ex-
piating these poetical trespasses on this side of
purgatory. Nay, more, if it rests with me to
direct your future lucubrations, I shall certainly
urge you to a repetition of the same conduct—
on purpose to show what an admirable knack
you have at confession and reformation; and
so without more hesitation I shall venture to
recommend the muse not to be restrained by ill-
grounded timidity, but to go on and prosper.
You see, madam, when once the woman has
tempted us and we have tasted the forbidden
fruit, there is no such thing as checking our
appetite, whatever the consequences may be.
You will, I dare say, recognise our being genuine
descendants of those who are reputed to be our
progenitors. Before I come to a more serious
conclusion of my letter I must beg leave to say
a word or two about these fine things you have
been telling in such harmonious and beautiful
numbers. Fiction is to be sure the very life and
soul of poetry. All poets and poetesses have
been indulged in the free and indisputable use of
it—time out of mind, and to oblige you to make

such an excellent poem on such a subject without any materials but those of simple reality would be as cruel as the edicts of Pharaoh, which compelled the Children of Israel to manufacture bricks without the necessary ingredients. Thus are you sheltered under the authority of prescription, and I will not dare to charge you with an intentional breach of the rules of the decalogue in giving so bright a colouring to the service I have been enabled to render my country, though I am not conscious of deserving more at your hands than what the poorest and most disinterested friendship has a right to claim: actuated by which you will permit me to thank you in a most affectionate manner for the kind wishes you have so happily expressed for me and the partner of all my domestic enjoyments. Be assured we can never forget our friend at Morven and that I am, my dear madam, your most obedient and obliged servant,

Go. Washington.

Elizabeth Montgomery Witherspoon

Rev. John Witherspoon, D.D.,[13] who became President of Princeton College and a signer of the Declaration of Independence, was married

to Elizabeth Montgomery in Scotland, shortly
after completing his education in Edinburgh
University, in 1743. His biographers say of her:
"She was a Scotch woman of little education,
but whose piety, benevolence, and graciousness
made her beloved by all who knew her. Dr.
Witherspoon (sometimes spelled Wotherspoon)
was the son of a minister descended from John
Knox, the great Covenanter, and as a young man,
had established a wide reputation for learning
and other sterling qualities. He was offered the
presidency of Princeton in 1766 but declined because of financial embarrassments and the opposition of his wife who did not wish to leave her
family and friends and journey into a strange
land. In 1768, Richard Stockton, then travelling
in Scotland, visited Dr. Witherspoon and, acting
for the trustees, again urged his acceptance. His
arguments prevailed and Dr. Witherspoon and
his family arrived in Princeton, in August, 1768.

The Witherspoons had ten children, five of
whom died before they left Scotland; three sons
and two daughters accompanied their parents
to America. James, the eldest, a young man of
great promise graduated from Princeton in 1770,
and joined the American army as an aide to

General Nash, with the rank of major. He was killed at the battle of Germantown, Oct. 4, 1777. John, the second son, graduated from Princeton in 1774, practised medicine in South Carolina, and was lost at sea in 1795. David, the youngest son, graduated the same year as his brother, married the widow of General Nash, and practised law in New Berne, N. C.

Anna, the eldest daughter, married Rev. Samuel Smith, D.D., who succeeded Dr. Witherspoon as President of Princeton. Frances, the youngest daughter, married Dr. David Ramsey, the historian of South Carolina.

Elizabeth Montgomery Witherspoon died in 1789. Eighteen months later, Dr. Witherspoon married the young widow of Dr. Dill of Philadelphia, aged twenty-three. Their daughter married Rev. James S. Woods of Pennsylvania.

Ann Borden Hopkinson

In the Pennsylvania *Chronicle and Universal Advertiser*, of Monday, September 5, 1768, appeared the following wedding announcement:

"BORDENTOWN, Sept. 3.

"On Thursday last FRANCIS HOPKINSON, ESQ., of Philadelphia, was joined in the Velvet Bonds

of Hymen, to Miss NANCY BORDEN, of this place,
a lady amiable both for her internal as well as her
external Accomplishments and in the Words of a
celebrated Poet:

> 'Without all shining, and within all white,
> Pure to the sense, and pleasing to the sight.' "

Ann Borden, who married Francis Hopkinson
in Christ Church, Bordentown, Sept. 1, 1768, was
the daughter of Judge Joseph Borden, a prominent and wealthy citizen of New Jersey. He
was proprietor of a boat and stage line running
from Philadelphia to New York, and during the
Revolutionary period an active patriot, member
of the first Revolutionary Convention which
met in New Brunswick in 1774, and of various
committees afterward. His son, Captain Joseph
Borden, brother to Mrs. Hopkinson, raised and
commanded the Burlington County troop of
light horse.

Nancy Borden, as she was usually called, was
a handsome, vivacious girl, well educated for the
times and highly accomplished. She and her
sister Maria, who married Thomas McKean, also
a signer and afterward Governor of Pennsylvania,
were said to have been the most beautiful women

of New Jersey. She seems to have been admirably fitted to be the life companion of the brilliant young lawyer who was both poet and musician as well as man of affairs. After his marriage, Hopkinson took up his residence in Bordentown and began the practice of law. He was a member of the Provincial Convention at New Brunswick in 1774, and of the first Continental Congress as a delegate from New Jersey, and afterward, Chief Justice of the State. He maintained his home in Philadelphia, and a handsome country place at Bordentown where he and his family lived until 1779, when he returned to Philadelphia to take up his duties as Judge of the Court of Admiralty. He was a delegate to the Constitutional Convention of 1787 and by appointment of President Washington, Judge of the United States District Court for Pennsylvania, in 1789. He died in 1791, in the fifty-third year of his age. His wife survived him thirty-six years, dying in 1827.

The children of Ann and Francis Hopkinson were as follows: James, Joseph, Elizabeth, Maria, Thomas, Ann, a second Thomas, Francis, and Sarah Johnson. Of these James and both Thomases died in infancy. The others all mar-

ried. Joseph, the oldest son was born in 1770.
He was a man of great ability and won distinction in the law, being United States Court Judge,
under appointment by President Adams, at
the time of his death. He will be longest remembered, however, as the author of *Hail Columbia*,
which he wrote in 1798. Elizabeth Hopkinson
married Jonathan Williams Condy, a prominent
Philadelphia lawyer and member of Congress.
Mary Hopkinson married Isaac Smith[14] of Ac-
comac County, Virginia; her sister Ann, the
"signer's" sixth child married Ebenezer Stout
of Trenton, N. J. The youngest of Francis
Hopkinson's sons, Francis, Jr., married Mary
Hewitt, *née* Morton.

Deborah Scudder Hart

Deborah Scudder Hart, wife of John Hart, was
the youngest daughter of Richard B. Scudder
and his wife, Hannah Reeder Scudder, who had
come to New Jersey about 1717, and settled on
the Delaware River near the Falls. She married
John Hart, a farmer of Hunterdon County, in
1740, and thirteen children were born to them,
nearly all of whom lived to become men and
women.

John Hart was generally known as "Honest John," and he was a grey-haired old man when he was sent as a delegate to the first Continental Congress, where he was an active and outspoken advocate of political liberty. Soon after the Declaration of Independence, New Jersey became the theatre of war. The progress of the British troops and their Tory allies was marked by rapine and wanton destruction of property. Mr. Hart was away from home in attendance upon Congress and the two oldest sons were in the Continental army. Mrs. Hart was suffering from a disease that would not allow of her being removed to any great distance. Her children carried her to a place of safety and left their home to be pillaged and destroyed by the Hessians and Tories. Mr. Hart hurried home from Congress to his dying wife—for anxiety and exposure had been too much for her wasted strength and she was dying. It was but a short time that he was given to sit by her bedside, before he was forced to fly. He was a marked man and for weeks he was hunted by the Tories like a criminal. Those were dark days for Deborah Hart. While Washington's fast dwindling army was lying inactive, her home in ruins,

and her husband a fugitive, she lay on her death-
bed cheerful and trusting in the God of her
fathers that the right would yet prevail. And
so she died, October 28, 1776, while John Hart,
that staunch old patriot, was carrying his grey
hairs and the physical infirmities of sixty-eight
years from one hiding-place to another; for weeks
scarcely ever sleeping the second night under the
same roof because of the danger it brought the
owner of that roof to harbour him. There came
a night of snow and rain when he had not the
place to lay his head. He knocked at a cabin
door and was refused admission and he was too
tired to go farther. The storm was increasing,
and he was glad to crawl into an empty stable,
used as a dog kennel and rest until morning.

Then came the battle of Trenton and the
capture of Rahl's Hessians. Again the skies of
New Jersey began to clear and old John Hart
and his scattered flock gathered around their
ruined hearthstone and prepared to build up a
new home. His personal losses had been heavy,
and his health badly broken by his hardships,
but he ever remained the same ardent and
earnest champion of independence until his
death which occurred in 1780.

The children born to Deborah and John Hart were: Sarah, Jesse, Martha, Nathaniel, John, Susannah, Mary, Abigail, Edward, Scudder, Daniel, and Deborah. One child died in infancy, unnamed. It is said that the known descendants of John Hart may be found in every State in the Union.

Sarah Hatfield Clark

Sarah Hatfield, was the eldest daughter of Isaac Hatfield[15] of Elizabethtown, N. J., and was born in 1728. She was a sister of Elder Isaac Hatfield and a first cousin of Mrs. Robert Ogden, mother of General Mathias Ogden and Governor Aaron Ogden. Further than this but little has come down to us of her or her family except that the Hatfields were well-to-do and respectable people of Essex County.

She was twenty-one years old when she was married to Abraham Clark, a young farmer who had studied surveying which he practised along with looking after his farm. He had also made some study of law though never admitted to the bar and was known as "the poor man's lawyer," because of his ready advice to his neighbours who were not able to carry their troubles to higher

priced counsellors. Under the Colonial government Clark held the offices of Sheriff of Essex
County and Clerk of the Assembly, and from his
prominence in the northern part of the Colony
as well as his known sympathy with the movement was sent as a delegate to the Continental
Congress that enacted the Declaration of Independence, and continued a member of that body
for many years.

Sarah Clark was not called upon to bear some
of the burdens that fell to the lot of Annis
Stockton or Deborah Hart, as her home was not
in the path of the invading army, but two of her
sons who were officers in the Continental army
were captured by the British and imprisoned
in New York. Because of the activity of the
father, the sons were most inhumanly treated.
Thomas Clark, the eldest son, a captain of
artillery was at one time immured in a dungeon
without food for days, except what his fellow
prisoners were able to pass in to him through a
keyhole. The second son, Isaac, suffered terribly
from the rigours of his confinement. It was not
until this was reported in Congress and measures
taken to retaliate upon two British captains,
held by the Americans, that the treatment of the

Clarks was mitigated and their exchange brought about.

Abraham Clark died of sunstroke at Rahway in 1794, and his wife survived him about ten years. Both are buried at Rahway.

NOTES TO CHAPTER I

[1] Written to celebrate the unveiling of a monument to Dr. Josiah Bartlett, erected in Amesbury, Mass., where he was born.

[2] "In 1707, Joseph Bartlett was drafted and sent with others to Haverhill to defend the town against an expected attack of French and Indians from Canada. August 29, 1708, about 160 French and 50 Indians attacked the town and set fire to several buildings. Mr. Bartlett and others were in a chamber of Captain Wainright's house from the windows of which they fired upon the enemy. They were informed that their only safety was in surrender. Mr. Bartlett secreted his gun in the chimney above the fireplace, went down, asked for quarter, was bound, and carried to Canada where he remained a prisoner until he was redeemed. After a captivity of four years he returned. He afterward visited Haverhill and found his gun where he had secreted it. It finally came to his grand nephew, Richard Bartlett of Amesbury, Mass., who carried it while a soldier in the Revolutionary War. Richard brought the gun back with him from the Revolution and it was afterward blown to pieces by some boy celebrating Fourth of July. Levi Bartlett (author of this sketch) collected the fragments in 1879, and riveted, and wired the gun together and deposited it in the rooms of the New Hampshire Historical Society where it may still be seen."

[3] Mrs. Clyde, a niece of Matthew Thornton (signer) fled from Indians into the woods with her eight children, one a babe in arms. She hid for twenty-four hours behind logs, near where Indians were passing. Exhibiting wonderful strength and endurance she finally reached the fort in safety.—*American Monthly Magazine.*

[4] Abigail and Blanche were daughters of Rev. William Smith. They had as suitors, the Rev. Zedadiah Chapman and John Adams. The young, handsome, and accomplished clergyman was acceptable to the father; his horse had the best of care and every attention was

paid to him. The horse of the young lawyer who came to see Abigail did not fare so well but stood the whole evening, shivering unprotected. When Blanche went to ask her father's consent to her marriage to the Rev. Mr. Chapman, his reply was: "You have my cordial approval, my child. Mr. Chapman will have a warm welcome in our home circle. Now choose a text, child, and I will preach you a sermon. "Father," said Blanche, " this is my text, ' For Mary hath chosen that good part which shall not be taken from her.'" Young Abigail approached more timidly, when the time came for her to ask for his approval of her marriage to her lively young suitor. When his reluctant consent was given, he could do no less than preach her a sermon also. "Father," said Abigail, "I know that you will preach a sermon for me." The father said he would if she would select the text. "This is my text," she said, "And John came neither eating nor drinking and ye say he hath a devil."—From anecdotes of Rev. Mr. Chapman.

⁵ Charles Francis Adams, grandson of Abigail Adams.

⁶ *American Statesman* series.

⁷ John Hancock had Copley, the artist, paint Samuel Adams's picture for him as he appeared before Governor Hutchinson after the Boston Massacre. The picture hung for many years in the Hancock mansion in Beacon Street, Boston, and is now in the Art Museum alongside that of John Hancock, painted by the same artist.

⁸ From sketch accompanying *Works of Robert Treat Paine, Jr., Esq.*, by Charles Prentiss, of Boston, printed and published by J. Belcher in 1812.

⁹ Hon. Elbridge Gerry of New York, for many years president of the Society for the Prevention of Vice, is a grandson of the signer.

¹⁰ James Schoolcraft Sherman, Vice-President of the United States, is a lineal descendant of Roger Sherman.

¹¹ In a memorandum, purporting to be in the handwriting of Governor Wolcott, now in possession of the Connecticut Historical Society, there is given a list of those who helped to melt up and make bullets of the leaden statue of George III, taken from Bowling Green, in 1776. The list which includes some of his own children is as follows: "Mrs. Marvin, 6,058; Ruth Marvin 11,592; Laura 8,378; Mary Ann 10,790; Frederick 936; Mrs. Beach 1,802; made by sundry persons 2,182; gave Litchfield militia on alarm 50; let the regiment of Col. Wigglesworth have 300."

[12] The name has been given in some histories as "Isabella" but the marriage license, secured by William Floyd, Aug. 20, 1760 (or '61, the date has been blurred) gives the name as "Hannah," and that is the name given in family traditions.

[13] Brigadier-General W. W. Wotherspoon, President of the Government's War College, and one of the greatest military authorities in the country, and who is a direct descendant of the "signer," spells his name "Wotherspoon," but the sturdy old President of Princeton College, who signed the Declaration, wrote it with an "i."

[14] A noted living descendant of Francis Hopkinson, the "signer," is Francis Hopkinson Smith, author and artist, who comes from this branch of the family.

[15] Samuel G. Arnold, in his *Biographies of Distinguished Jerseymen*, spells the name "Hetfield," and it is given in other publications as "Huffield," but Rev. Edwin E. Hatfield, in his *History of Elizabeth, N. J.*, spells the name as given above, and he is a direct descendant of Isaac Hatfield.

"HEROES, who render up their lives
     On the country's fiery altar stone,
They do not offer themselves alone;
What shall become of the soldier's wives?
They stay behind in their humble cots,
Weeding the humble garden spots,
Some to speed the needle and thread,
For the soldier's children must be fed;
All to sigh through the toilsome day,
And at night teach lisping lips to pray,
For the father marching far away."
                                    E. C. Stedman.

Chapter II

Wives of the Signers (*Continued*)

Winning personality and devoted patriotism of some of the notable women of the Central and Southern Colonies—Mary White Morris—Julia Stockton Rush—Deborah Read Franklin and her daughter Sarah Bache—Anne Justis Morton—Elizabeth Meredith Clymer—Eleanor Armor Smith—Ann Savage Taylor—Rachael Bird Wilson—Ann Lawlor Ross—Gertrude Ross Read—Mary Borden McKean—Ann Baldwin Chase—Margaret Brown Stone—Mary Darnell Carroll—Anne Lewis Wythe—Anne Aylett Lee—Martha Wayles Jefferson—Elizabeth Bassett Harrison—Lucy Grymes Nelson—Rebecca Tayloe Lee—Elizabeth Corbin Braxton—Ann Clark Hooper—Susan Lyme Penn—Harriet Middleton Rutledge—Elizabeth Mathews Heyward—Elizabeth Shubreck Lynch—Mary Izard Middleton—Mrs. Gwinnet—Abigail Burr Hall—Dorothy Camber Walton.

MARY White, who afterward became the wife of Robert Morris, the great financier of the Revolutionary War, was born April 13, 1749, the youngest child of Thomas and Esther White of Philadelphia. That she was well educated and carefully trained in the accomplishments of her day, is evidenced by the social position she so gracefully filled

in after life and by the literary style of such of
her letters as remain to us. She was prominent
in Philadelphia society before her marriage and
is referred to in the opening stanza of Col.
Sheppen's *Lines Written in an Assembly Room*
designed to commemorate the beauty and charms
of Philadelphia's belles:

> " In lovely White's most pleasing form,
>   What various graces meet ;
>   How blest with every striking charm,
>   How languishingly sweet ! "

She was married to Robert Morris, March 2,
1769, by the Rev. Richard Peters. Her husband
was at the time thirty-five years old, and one
of the most prominent merchants of the day.
Maternal cares came early to Mary Morris,
her son Robert being born in December of the
same year as her marriage. The second child,
Thomas, was born February 26, 1771; then came
William White, born August 9, 1772, and their
oldest daughter, Hettie, was born July 30, 1774.

Toward the close of 1776, when the British
were approaching Philadelphia, Congress moved
to Baltimore. Mr. Morris remained in Philadelphia but sent Mrs. Morris to follow Congress
and visit her step-sister, Mrs. Hall, with whom

Mrs. Robert Morris.

(Mary White.)

From an engraving of the painting by C. W. Peale.

her father and mother were then staying. Here she remained for several months and her letters to her husband are of interest, giving as they do glimpses of her real character. On December 20th, she wrote:

". . . I long to give you an account of the many difficulties and uneasiness we have experienced in this journey. Indeed my spirits were very unable to the task after that greatest conflict, flying from home; the sufferings of our dear little Tom distressed us all, and without the affectionate assistance of Mr. Hall and the skilfulness of Dr. Cole, whose services I shall never forget, I don't know what might have been the consequence, as it was a boil of an uncommon nature and required the surgeon's hand. We had reason to apprehend, too, we should lose our goods. The many circumstances of this affair I must leave till I see you, as neither my patience nor my paper will hold out. . . . But after all the dangers, I 've the pleasure to inform you we are safely housed in this hospitable mansion. . . . I thought I was prepared for every misfortune; for, as you observe, of late we have little else. Yet, when Lee is taken prisoner (Gen. Charles Lee at Basking Ridge), who is proof against those feelings his loss must occasion?"

On December 30th, on receipt of the news of the victory of Trenton, she wrote to her husband: ". . . We had been for many days impatiently wishing for a letter from you, as the news we hear from any other quarter is not to be depended upon; but when the welcome one arrived, which brought those glad tidings, it more than compensated for what our unfortunate circumstances prepared our minds to expect. . . . but I hope, indeed, the tide is turned, and that our great Washington will have the success his virtues deserve, and rout the impious army who, from no other principle but that of enslaving this once happy country, have prosecuted this Cruell war, . . ."

After hearing of the Battle of Princeton, she wrote on January 15, 1777: ". . . I tryed to be cheerful; how could I be really so when hourly in expectation of hearing the determination of so important a Battle, and when the express arrived and pronounced Washington victorious, would you believe it, your Molly could not join in the general rejoicing? No! nor never can at a victory so dearly bought. . . ."

In March, 1777, Mrs. Morris returned to Philadelphia. Evidently the separation from her husband and the worries and anxieties she had experienced had impaired her health, for in a letter written to her "Mama" on March 15th and addressed to "Mrs. White, at Aqula Hall's, Esqr., near Bush Town, Maryland," she writes: "I suppose Jemmy Hall has told you how everybody exclaims at my thinness; several of my acquaintances did not know me till they had time to recollect and then declared there was very little traces of my former self. . . ."

In a postscript to this same letter, she adds: "Billy has been told that Congress appointed him their Chaplain when in Baltimore, but has not yet heard it from them, and begs it may not be mentioned." "Billy" was her brother, the future eminent prelate and father of the Protestant Episcopal Church in this country, Bishop William White.

Mrs. Morris had not been at her home a month before fears of Howe's approach made it necessary to move again. On April 14, 1777, she wrote her mother: ". . . We are preparing for another flight in packing up our furniture, and removing them to a new purchase, Mr. Morris has made ten miles from Lancaster. . . ."

A fortnight later, she writes: "I am yet on dear Philadelphia ground, but expect soon to inhabit the Hills, where we shall remain, if possible, in the enjoyment of all that is beautiful to the eye and grateful to the taste, . . . We intend sending off our best furniture in Lancaster with all the linen we can spare, and stores of all kinds, that our flight may be attended with as few incumbrances as possible."

In September, 1777, the near approach of the British Army obliged Congress to remove from Philadelphia, first to Lancaster and afterward to York, and at this time Mr. and Mrs. Morris removed to their country place, the Hills, where they remained until after the evacuation of the city by Sir Henry Clinton early in the summer of 1778. On July 2 of that year, Congress reassembled in Philadelphia. At this period, Benedict Arnold had command in the city, and Mrs. Morris, writing to her mother in November, said: "I know of no news, unless to tell you we are very gay, is such. . . . Tell Mr. Hall, even our military gentlemen

here are too liberal to make any distinctions between Whig and Tory ladyes—if they make any,
it is in the favour of the latter.   Such, strange
as it may seem, is the way those things are
conducted at present in this city.   It originates
at Headquarters and that I may make some
apology for such strange conduct, I must tell
you that cupid had given our little general a
more mortal wound than all the host of Britons
could, unless his present conduct can expiate
for his past—Miss Peggy Shippen is the fair
one."

In September, 1779, Mrs. Morris was called
upon to mourn the loss of her father, Col.
Thomas White, who died on the 29th. inst.

Early in the year 1781, Robert Morris was
made Superintendent of Finance.   He was supreme in his position, appointing and removing
subordinates, etc., at his own discretion.   This
power, combined with his wealth and social
position, gave him considerable prominence,
which was shared by his wife.   Their home was
visited by all the distinguished men of the time,
including a number of illustrious foreigners,
Prince de Broglie, Luzerne, the French Minister,
the Marquis de Chastellux, and others.   Luzerne

was on terms of the utmost intimacy with the Morris family and there is extant an invitation to Mr. and Mrs. Morris and Catharine Livingston, daughter of Governor Livingston of New Jersey, "together with the young family of Mrs. Morris," to dine at Shoemaker's Place on the following Saturday afternoon. It was from this French nobleman that Robert Morris borrowed, on his personal credit, twenty thousand pounds in specie, which he sent to Washington, and it was this money which enabled the great Commander to compel the capitulation of Cornwallis at Yorktown.

It was to Mr. Morris and his wife, that the honour fell of entertaining Washington in the latter end of the summer of 1781, when the General, accompanied by Count de Rochambeau and other foreign and American officers passed through Philadelphia on their way to join La Fayette near Yorktown, where they hoped, with the aid of De Grasse, who was hourly expected with his fleet, to capture Cornwallis and his army.

It was in the fall of 1781 that Mrs. Morris's two eldest sons, Robert, aged 12, and Thomas, aged 10, were sent to Europe to be educated,

the Revolution having made such matters difficult in this country. In the latter part of May,
1887, when the convention met to frame a constitution for the United States, Mrs. Morris again
had the honour of entertaining General Washington. Mr. Morris, who eleven years before
had signed the Declaration of Independence,
was a member of this convention, and it was
upon his motion that Washington was selected
to preside over the proceedings. Washington
made his home with the Morrises during the
entire time he was attending this convention.
When Washington was inaugurated the first
time, Mrs. Washington did not accompany him
to New York, but on Tuesday, May 19th, accompanied by her grandchildren, Eleanor and
George Washington Parke Custis, set out in
her private carriage for the seat of government.
She received ovations all along her route, and
on Thursday when she reached Gray's Ferry,
just outside of the city, she was met by Mrs.
Morris, whose guest she was to be, and accompanied by her entered the city escorted by a
large concourse of military and citizens amid
great demonstration.

Mrs. Washington remained with Mrs. Morris

until the following Monday, when she departed for New York, taking Mrs. Morris and her daughter Maria in her carriage as her guests. They were met on Wednesday at Elizabethtown by the President and Mr. Morris, and crossed over to New York on the President's barge. On Friday, May 29th, Mrs. Washington gave her first levee, at which Mrs. Morris was present, occupying the first place on her right, and in all her subsequent levees in New York and afterward in Philadelphia, when present, Mrs. Morris occupied this place of honour.

Mrs. Morris remained in New York with her husband until July 5th, when she returned to Philadelphia, Mr. Morris being detained in New York by his senatorial duties. It was mainly through his efforts that the seat of government was moved the following year to Philadelphia. As soon as it was definitely settled, Mr. Morris offered his handsome residence, the finest in the city, for the presidential mansion. The relations between the Washingtons and the Morrises were of the warmest. When Washington was elected President, he offered the Treasury[1] portfolio to Morris who declined it, but recommended Alexander Hamilton, who was appointed.

The history of the unfortunate wild land speculation of Morris, which wrecked his fortune and afforded the most unhappy chapter in the life of Mary Morris, is too well known to need retelling here. On February 15, 1798, he was arrested and next day taken to the debtors' department of the old Prune Street Prison, where he remained three years and a half, until liberated, in 1801, by the General Bankrupt law. It was in October of this year that William Morris, third son of Mary and Robert Morris, died of the malignant fever, in his twenty-seventh year.

During the confinement of Mr. Morris, his devoted wife and daughter Maria were his almost constant companions. Day after day Mrs. Morris visited the prison and dined at the cell table of her unfortunate husband, and while the malignant fever raged terribly in Prune Street, and infested the city, she never left him but continued her daily visits, though she had to walk through two rows of coffins piled from floor to ceiling of the room which adjoined his.

It was through the instrumentality of Gouverneur Morris, who though not a relative was one of the most intimate friends of Robert

Morris, that Mrs. Morris was kept from absolute want during the incarceration of her
husband. The title to the four tracts of land,
containing three million three hundred thousand
acres, which had been conveyed to the Holland
Land Co. by Mr. Morris in 1792 and 1793,
proved defective and required confirming, for
which Gouverneur Morris compelled the company to pay Mrs. Morris an annuity of $1500
during her lifetime, and this was all that she
then had to live upon.

Robert Morris came out of prison a broken-
down old man and lived about five years,
dying in 1806. After his death, Mrs. Morris
removed to Chestnut Street above Tenth, on
the south side, where she passed the remainder
of her life. She was residing here when La
Fayette made his famous tour through the
country, in 1824. He arrived in Philadelphia
on Tuesday morning, September 29th, and was
tendered the greatest ovation of his visit.
On the evening of his arrival he called upon
Mrs. Morris, the first private visit that he made
in the city. He had not seen her before that
day in thirty-seven years, but in driving past
her house that afternoon noticed her at the

window and recognised her. At the personal request of General La Fayette, Mrs. Morris attended the grand Civic Ball, given in his honour at the new Chestnut Street Theatre on the night of Monday, October 5th. Mrs. Morris, who was sixty-seven years old at the time, was described as "tall, graceful, and commanding, with a stately dignity of manner."

Julia Stockton Rush

Julia Stockton was the eldest daughter of Richard Stockton, an eminent New Jersey patriot and signer of the Declaration of Independence, and his wife, the gifted Annis Boudinot Stockton. She was born March 2, 1759, at "Morven," the estate of Richard Stockton, near Princeton, N. J., and received as liberal an education as was open to women of her day, supplemented by association with the cultivated people whom her father and mother were wont to gather in their hospitable home.

She was married January 11, 1776, to Dr. Benjamin Rush of Philadelphia, already one of the prominent medical practitioners of his day, a writer of acknowledged ability on medical subjects, and a public-spirited citizen, held in high esteem by his fellow townsmen.

Dr. Rush in his memoirs pays this tribute to his wife: "Let me here bear testimony to the worth of this excellent woman. She fulfilled every duty as a wife, mother, and mistress with fidelity and integrity. To me she was always a sincere and honest friend; had I yielded to her advice upon many occasions, I should have known less distress from various causes in my journey through life. . . . May God reward and bless her with an easy and peaceful old age if she should survive me, and after death confer upon her immediate and eternal happiness!"

It was not alone in his published writings that Dr. Rush pays tribute to his wife. A great-grandson of Benjamin Rush,[2] writing to the authors, says: "I am afraid our forebears did not keep with accuracy the deeds of noble women in the days that truly tried the souls of both men and women. I spent last evening going over a mass of data, including a copy of the Commonplace Book or diary of my great-grandfather Benjamin Rush. She is spoken of everywhere as a devoted wife and mother and of her urging her husband to take more care of

Julia Stockton Rush.
From an oil painting.

himself during the terrible yellow-fever scourge of 1793, in Philadelphia, when, much against her wishes, she remained out of town with her children, yet by daily letters encouraged Dr. Rush in his great work for humanity."

Thirteen children were born to Dr. Rush and his wife, as follows: John, Anne, Emily, Richard, Susannah, Elizabeth, Mary, James, William, Benjamin, a second Benjamin, Julia, Samuel, and a second William. Four died in infancy, Susannah, Elizabeth, the first Benjamin, and the first William. John Rush, who was a lieutenant in the U. S. Navy, died unmarried. Emily, the eldest daughter, married Ross Cuthbert, a young Canadian who had been graduated from Princeton and who afterward won distinction in Provincial affairs. Richard Rush, the third child, was Attorney-General of Pennsylvania, Attorney-General of the United States, Minister to Great Britain, Secretary of the Treasury, Minister to France, and unsuccessful candidate for the vice-presidency. He was married to Catharine Eliza Murray of Maryland, who bore him ten children. Julia Stockton Rush, a grandchild, married John Calvert, a lawyer of Maryland and a descendant of George

Calvert, first Lord Baltimore. James Rush, the third son of the "signer," became a noted medical authority and a writer, succeeded his father as Treasurer of the U. S. Mint, and endowed the "Ridgway" branch of the Philadelphia library. He was the husband of Phebe Ridgway Rush, for many years a leader of Philadelphia society and one of the most famous women in America. They died childless. Benjamin Rush, the sixth son of the "signer," died unmarried, and Julia the next child, who married Henry Jonathan Williams, a prominent member of the bar, died childless; Samuel Rush, the twelfth child, became a prominent attorney and married Anne Wilmer. The thirteenth child, William Rush, was a physician and married Elizabeth Fox Roberts.

Mrs. Rush died at their country seat, "Sydenham" (now Fifteenth Street and Columbus Ave., Philadelphia), July 7, 1848, and was buried in the grave of her husband in Christ Church burying ground, south-east corner Fifth and Arch streets, Philadelphia.

Deborah Read Franklin

Deborah Read, who became the wife of Benjamin Franklin, September 1, 1730, was a

Deborah Read (**Mrs. Benjamin Franklin**).
From an engraving of the painting owned by Prof. Hodge.

native of Philadelphia, though her people do not seem to have been of enough prominence to have left any particular record in its annals. She was about twenty-five years old at the time of the marriage—a few months older than her husband.

Franklin, in his *Autobiography*, has told the story of their first meeting, that memorable Sunday morning, in October, 1723, when Franklin, then a lad of seventeen, with a loaf of bread under each arm and munching a third, walked "up Market Street as far as Fourth, passing by the door of Mr. Read, my future wife's father; when she, standing at the door, saw me and thought I made, as I most certainly did, a most awkward, ridiculous appearance."

A few months afterward, when Franklin had established himself as a printer, he became acquainted with Miss Read, and when he went to England on Governor Sir William Keith's wild-goose chase he was engaged to her. He seems to have half forgotten her, however, as he wrote to her but once. Miss Deborah herself was easily comforted, as soon after Franklin's departure she married one "Rogers, a potter." Rogers seems to have been a poor

stick for he deserted his young wife in a short
time and departed leaving only his debts behind.
The news of his death must have been welcome
to his wife as there were stories afloat that he
had another wife living.

Deborah Read seems to have made Franklin
a most excellent wife and they lived happily
together for forty years. "None of the inconveniences happened that we had apprehended,"
he wrote; "she proved a good and faithful
helpmeet; assisted me much by attending the
shop; we throve together and have mutually
endeavoured to make each other happy."

"Mrs. Franklin was a handsome woman of
comely figure," writes Franklin's biographer,
"yet nevertheless an industrious and frugal one;
later on in life he boasted that he had been
clothed from head to foot in linen of his wife's
manufacture. An early contribution of his own
to the domestic menage was his illegitimate son,
William, born, soon after his wedding, of a mother
of whom no record or tradition remains. It
was an unconventional wedding gift to bring
home to a bride; but Mrs. Franklin, with a
breadth and liberality of mind akin to her
husband's, readily took the babe, not only to her

home but really to her heart, and reared him as if he had been her own offspring."

Two children were born to Deborah Read Franklin, a son who died in infancy and a daughter who grew to womanhood. Mrs. Franklin died of paralysis in December, 1774, while her husband was still in England as agent of the Province of Pennsylvania. Because of the fact that Sarah Franklin, the daughter, was called upon to take her mother's place as homemaker before the Revolution, as well as for her own patriotism and public spirit, it may not be out of place to consider her in this chapter.

Sarah Franklin Bache

One of the most popular women of her day in her native city was Sarah Franklin. She was born in 1744 and carefully educated by her father—probably as broadly educated as any woman in the Colony. As a girl, she is said to have been plain, almost to ugliness, but with a sense of humour and a play of wit which together with her good nature and kindliness made her generally popular.

Of her girlhood there is but little to tell, so

smooth was the flow of the current of her life, until she reached her twentieth year, at which time her father was sent to England in a representative capacity. The incident leading up to this was about the first introduction of the young woman in politics, a subject which ever after held for her the keenest interest.

William Penn's sons had drawn away from the Quakers, of whom their father had been a leader, and joined the Church of England, a large majority of whose members were of the Proprietary Party. Most of the Quakers were in opposition to this party and with this opposition Dr. Franklin had acted. After fourteen years' service as member of the Lower House of the State Legislature, he was defeated by a few votes in 1764. His friends, who were in the majority in the Upper House, immediately elected him as agent for the Province in England. To this appointment, the Proprietary Party took great exceptions. Church and State were much more closely knit together in those days than now, and the fight was carried right into Christ Church, where Franklin was a pewholder and Mrs. Franklin and her daughter were communicants. Consequently, when the young woman found a remonstrance against the appointment of her father laid on the communion table of her church for signatures, she was indignant and made no attempt to hide her feelings at this "outrage against decency and the feelings of her family," and threatened to leave the church and congregation. It was upon this occasion that her father wrote to her from Reedy Island, in November, as he was on his way to Europe: "Go constantly to the church, whoever preaches. The act of devotion in the common prayer book is your principal business there; and if properly attended to will do more toward amending the heart than sermons can do; for they were composed by men of much greater piety and wisdom than our common composers of sermons can pretend to be; and therefore I prefer you would never miss the prayer days. Yet I do not mean that you should despise sermons, even of preachers you dislike, for the discourse is often much sweeter than the man, as sweet and clear waters come through very dirty earth. I am more particular on this head, as you seemed to express, a little before I left, some inclination to leave our church, which I would not have you do."

Some of Miss Franklin's letters to her father during his absence in England have been preserved and are most interesting, as showing not only an insight into the strong feeling that agitated the American people of the day, but the delightful yet respectful affection and intimacy between father and daughter that existed. In her first letter she says:

". . . The subject is the Stamp Act and nothing else is talked of. The Dutch talk of 'tamp tack' and the negroes of the 'tamp,' in short everybody has something to say." The letter closes with: "There is not a young lady of my acquaintance but what desires to be remembered to you. I am, my dear, your very dutiful daughter, Sally Franklin."

In the following year, March, 1765, she writes: "We have heard in a roundabout way that the Stamp Act is repealed. The people are determined to believe it, though it came from Ireland to Maryland. The bells rung, we had bonfires and one house was illuminated. I never heard so much noise in my life; the children seem distracted. I hope and pray the report may be true."

Sarah Franklin was married in October, 1767,

Sarah Franklin Bache.
From the engraving by Burt.

to Richard Bache, a merchant of Philadelphia, who had come to the Colony several years before from Yorkshire, England, and who seems to have been a substantial sort of citizen in many ways and a good American when the time came. For several years Mr. and Mrs. Bache lived with Mrs. Franklin until her death.

When the British were approaching Philadelphia, in 1776, through New Jersey, Mr. Bache removed his family to Goshen township, Chester County. Dr. Franklin was at that time Minister to France, having been sent by the Continental Congress in the previous October. With him had also gone his eldest grandson, Temple Bache, to begin his education. Mrs. Bache's letter to her father has been preserved. She wrote to him from their home in Goshen, February 23, 1777, as follows:

"We have been impatiently waiting to hear of your arrival for some time. It was seventeen weeks yesterday since you left us—a day I shall never forget. How happy we shall all be to hear you are all safe arrived and well. You had not left us long before we were obliged to leave town. I shall never forget nor forgive them for turning me out of house and home in midwinter and we are still about twenty-four miles from Philadelphia, in Chester County, the next plantation to where Mr. Ashbridge used to live. We have two comfortable rooms and are as happily situated as I can be, separated from Mr. Bache; he comes to see us as often as his business will permit. Your library we sent out of town well packed in boxes, a week before us, and all the valuable things, mahogany excepted, we brought with us. There was such confusion that it was a hard matter to get out at any rate; when we shall get back again I know not, though things are altered much in our favour, since we left town. I think I shall never be afraid of staying in it again, if the enemy were only three miles away instead of thirty, since 'our cowards,' as Lord Sandwich calls them, are so ready to turn out against those heroes who were to conquer all before them, but have found themselves so much mistaken; their courage never brought them to Trenton, till they heard our army was disbanded. I send the newspapers; but as they do not always speak true and as there may be some particulars in Mr. Bache's letters to me that are not in them, I will copy those parts of his letters that contain the news. I think you will have it more regular."

A short time after, Mrs. Bache and her family returned to Philadelphia, but in September, a few days after the birth of her eldest daughter, she again left town, staying for a time with friends in Bucks County and then taking up her residence in Lancaster County where she remained until the British left Philadelphia. On July 14, 1778, she wrote to Dr. Franklin:

"Once more I have the happiness of addressing you from this dearly beloved city, after having been kept out of it more than nine months. . . . I found your house and furniture in much better order than I had reason to expect from such a rapacious crew; they stole and carried off with them some of your musical instruments, viz: a Welsh harp, ball harp, the set of tuned bells which were in a box, viol-de-gamba, all the spare armonica glasses, one or two spare cases. Your armonica is safe. They took likewise a few books that were left behind, the chief of which were Temple's school books and the *History of the Arts and Sciences* in French, which is a great loss to the public; some of your electric apparatus is missing also—

a Captain André took with him the picture of you that hung in the dining-room. The rest of the pictures are safe and met with no accident except the frame of Alfred, which is broken to pieces."

The André mentioned was Major André who was quartered in Dr. Franklin's house during the British occupation of the city. In a letter written in October, when Mrs. Bache and her family had returned to the city, after passing the summer at Manheim, in Lancaster County, she says: "This is the first opportunity I have had since my return home of writing to you. We found our furniture in much better order than we could expect, which was owing to the care that Miss Clifton took of all we left behind; my being removed four days after my little girl was born, made it impossible for me to remove half the things we did in our former flight."

After describing her little girl, Mrs. Bache continues: "I would give a good deal if you could see her; you can't think how fond of kissing she is, and she gives such old-fashioned smacks, General Arnold says that he would give a good deal to have her for a school mistress to teach the young ladies how to kiss. . . .

There is hardly such a thing as living in town, everything is so high. If I were to mention the prices of the common necessaries of life it would astonish you. I can scarcely believe that I am in Philadelphia. . . . They really asked six dollars for a pair of gloves, and I have been obliged to pay fifteen pounds for a common calimanco petticoat without quilting, that I once could have got for fifteen shillings." This depreciation in Continental currency continued until Mrs. Bache, writing in a spirit of amused levity, says that she has to send her servant to market "with two baskets, one to hold her purchases and the other to carry the money with which to pay for them."

In a letter written in January, 1779, Mrs. Bache, after further comments on the continued high prices, goes on: "There never was so much dressing and pleasure going on; old friends meeting again, the Whigs in high spirits and strangers of distinction among us." She speaks of having met General and Mrs. Washington several times and adds: "He always inquires after you in the most affectionate manner and speaks of you highly. We danced at Mrs. Powell's on your birthday, or night I should say, in company together, and he told me it was the anniversary of his marriage,—it was just twenty years that night."

In the movement of the patriotic ladies of Philadelphia in 1780 to furnish food and clothing for destitute soldiers, Mrs. Bache was one of the leading spirits, and after the death of Mrs. Esther Reed the duty of collecting the contributions and distributing the funds was largely carried on by her and four other members of the Executive Committee. When it was proposed to present the money raised, "a hard dollar to each man," General Washington advised against it and pointed out that, most of all, the soldiers needed clothing, "especially shirts." So the fund was devoted to the buying of linen out of which the women themselves cut and made twenty-two hundred shirts. These shirts were cut out at Mrs. Bache's house.

A letter from M. de Marbois to Dr. Franklin, the succeeding year, speaks of Mrs. Bache: "If there are in Europe any women who need a model of attachment to domestic duties and love for their country, Mrs. Bache may be pointed out to them as such. She passed a part of last year in exertions to rouse the zeal of the Pennsylvania ladies, and she made on the occasion such a happy use of the eloquence which, you know, she possesses, that a large part of the American army was provided with shirts bought with their money or made by their hands. In her application for this purpose, she showed the most indefatigable zeal, the most unwearied perseverance, and a courage in asking, which surpassed even the obstinate reluctance of the Quakers in refusing."

The closing years of Mrs. Bache's life were peaceful and pleasant in the main. Dr. Franklin returned from the Court of France in September, 1785, after an absence of seven years, loaded with honours at home and abroad, to spend the remaining years of his life in the family of his daughter and among the descendants of the friends of his early days. In 1792, Mr. and Mrs. Bache visited England, spending nearly a year. Two years later, Mr. Bache retired from business and removed his family to his farm on the Delaware River about sixteen miles from Philadelphia. Here they spent thirteen years, noted for their hospitality. In 1807, Mr. Bache removed to Philadelphia for the sake of securing better medical attendance for his wife, who had

recently developed cancer. The disease, however, proved incurable and she passed away
in October, 1808, aged sixty-four years. She
was the mother of eight children, of whom one,
a daughter, died in childhood. Her eldest son
died in 1798 of yellow fever.[3]

Anne Justis Morton

When Anne Justis married John Morton in
1745, or 1746, she probably had little idea of
the honours the future held in store for her youth-
ful husband, even though he was already looked
upon in their little community as a young man
with a promising future.

They were of neighbouring farmer folk in
Chester County, now Delaware County, Pennsylvania. Both were of Swedish extraction,
their forebears having been of that tide of
immigration which poured into the "lower
counties" about the opening of the eighteenth
century. John Morton cultivated his own
patrimonial acres, but was able to alternate
his farm labours with surveying new lands,
having been taught that branch of mathematics
along with "accompting" by his step-father,
John Sketchley, an English gentleman who

married the Widow Morton while John was yet
an infant in arms. We find nothing more of
Anne Justis for many years. Her husband,
grown wealthy, seems to have won the respect
and confidence of his neighbours, for he was
commissioned as Justice of the Peace in 1764,
and within a few months elected to the Provincial Legislature, of which body he was Speaker for
a number of years. Later he was High Sheriff
of the county for three years, afterward presiding judge of the Provincial Court, and then
one of the judges of the Supreme Court.

During all these years Anne Justis was looking
after their estate and rearing their family of
children, of whom there were eight, three sons
and five daughters. In 1774, Mr. Morton was
sent as delegate to the Congress of Colonies in
Philadelphia, and was re-elected in 1775 and
again in 1776. It was the vote of John Morton,
when the delegates of Pennsylvania were equally
divided, that broke the tie and threw the voice
of the delegation for independence. The labours
and responsibilities of his career through this
trying period broke down his health, and in
April, 1777, he died in the fifty-fourth year of
his age.

The surviving children of John Morton were as follows: Aaron, the eldest, married Frances, daughter of Richard and Elizabeth Paschall Armitt. They lived in Delaware County for several years and afterward emigrated to Ohio. Sketchley, the second child, became a major in the Pennsylvania line of the Continental Army; he married Rebecca, daughter of John and Mary Neidermar Taylor and died in 1795. Dr. John became a surgeon in the Continental Army and died while a prisoner of war on the British prison ship *Falmouth* in New York harbour. The late John S. Morton of Springfield had in his possession a letter written by Dr. Morton to his father while he was a prisoner, in which he said they were "almost starved and could eat brickbats if they could get them." He died unmarried. Concerning Sarah and Lydia, nothing definite can be learned. Elizabeth died of consumption, unmarried. Mary married Charles Justis of Kingessing, and Ann, the youngest, married, in 1784, Captain John Davis of Chester County, who had fought through the Revolutionary War as an officer of the Pennsylvania line.

When the British Army passed through the

neighbourhood of his late residence, after the Battle of Brandywine, they despoiled his widow and children of property to the value of over one thousand dollars. Mr. and Mrs. Morton were members of St. James Church in the town of Chester, and their remains are said to be interred in the old churchyard.

Elizabeth Meredith Clymer

Elizabeth Meredith was the daughter of Reese Meredith, a prominent and wealthy merchant of Philadelphia for more than half a century prior to the Revolutionary period. She was a handsome accomplished girl of most exemplary character, and her marriage in March, 1765, was considered a highly advantageous union on both sides.[4]

George Clymer was twenty-seven years old at the time of his marriage, and his bride, several years his junior. Left an orphan at the age of seven, he had been brought up in the family of his mother's brother, William Coleman, who not only gave him a liberal education, including two years' training in his own counting room, but dying, left to him most of his considerable fortune. After completing his education, young Clymer went into the mercantile business and afterward formed a partnership with Reese Meredith and his son. It was soon after this that Mr. Clymer was married to Elizabeth Meredith. He was very public spirited and, during the Stamp Act agitation, began taking an active part in public affairs. He was at the head of a vigilance committee and afterward was a member of the Committee of Safety. In 1776 he was one of the delegates elected to the Continental Congress because of his pro-independence views and from that time practically gave up his private business to devote himself to public affairs. In Congress he was an indefatigable worker, whose cool judgment and unswerving patriotism were recognised on every side. Mr. Clymer seems to have been especi-ally obnoxious to the British. At the time of General Washington's defeat at Brandywine, when the British army was marching towards Philadelphia, Mr. Clymer's family retired for safety to their country home in Chester County. Tories led the enemy to their retreat. The house was sacked and the furniture destroyed; the wine cellars were raided and everything portable on the place was carried away. Upon this occasion Mrs. Clymer and her children saved themselves by a hasty flight back into the interior.

The married life of the Clymers was very harmonious and happy and only marred by the enforced separations and the hardships caused by the Revolution. Like most of the signers, he suffered large losses of property from British depredations. Eight children were born to Elizabeth and George Clymer, three of whom died in childhood. The others were: Henry, born in 1769, married Mary Willing; Meredith, who died unmarried; Margaret, who married George McCall; Nancy, who married Charles Lewis, and George who married Maria O'Brien; their son was Dr. Meredith Clymer a noted physician of Philadelphia and New York.

Eleanor Armor Smith

Eleanor Armor, of Newcastle, Delaware, "a young woman of many accomplishments and good family connection," became in 1745 or 1746, the wife of James Smith, of York County, Pennsylvania. Mr. Smith was a land surveyor and lawyer, who had a few months before removed from Shippensburg. He was the first

attorney to begin practice in York and remained
at the head of the bar of that county until after
the Revolution.

James Smith was born in Ireland and was
brought into Pennsylvania when a child, by
his father who settled on the Susquehanna.
He was educated in Philadelphia under Dr.
Allison, provost of the college, who taught him
Greek, Latin, and mathematics, including land
surveying. He studied law with an elder
brother who was established in practice at
Lancaster, after which he started in business
for himself at Shippensburg, then a thriving
town on the frontier. He prospered greatly,
but after a few years decided to remove to
York, where his family might have the advantages of a larger and more thickly settled
community. He was a rather eccentric character in some ways, one of his eccentricities being,
never to tell his age. His biographers have been
almost as reticent concerning his family, as the
dates of his marriage and of the births of his
children are all uncertain. Smith was endowed
with a vein of wit and humour, given to story
telling and jovial companionship.

Five children were born to James and Eleanor

Smith, three sons and two daughters. Only one of the sons and two of the daughters survived him. The son, James Smith, jr., died a few months after his father, and the daughter, became the wife of James Johnson, a prominent citizen of York.[5]

Long before the Revolution, Mr. Smith was pronounced in his views on the encroachment of the British ministry on the rights of the Colonies. He was a member of the Provincial Committee of Safety and upon the news from Lexington, organised a battalion around his own home, which elected him colonel, a position that, because of age, he was forced to decline. He was in the Continental Congress, in 1775, 1776, 1777, and 1778, after which he retired to continue the practice of his profession. Some of the letters which Colonel Smith wrote to his wife while in Congress have been preserved. Through them all runs a vein of drollery, a confidence in her ability to take care of their home affairs, and an air of affectionate comradeship that afford almost as much of an insight into her character as it does into his.

In a letter, written from Philadelphia, in October, 1776, he says: ". . . If Mr. Wilson should come through York, give him a flogging, he should have been here a week ago. I expect, however, to be home before election, my three months are nearly up. . . . This morning I put on the red jacket under my shirt. Yesterday I dined at Mr. Morris's and got wet going home, and my shoulder got troublesome, but by running a hot smoothing iron over it three times it got better—this is a new and cheap cure. My respects to all my friends and neighbours, my love to the children. I am your loving husband, James Smith."

The "Mr. Wilson" referred to above was his brother congressman, James Wilson, who had been attending court duties in Carlisle. In another letter dated "Congress Chamber," September 4, 1778, Mr. Smith writes:

". . . This morning I sent a bundle of Newspapers and a half finished letter by Mr. Hahn. Yesterday I dined with the President at his own home, he lives elegantly and keeps house himself, we had an elegant dinner and very good claret and madeira. . . . I am tired of the city heartily. It is very expensive living and not very agreeable; since I left the Indian Queen, I have paid for my room and bed, and breakfast and supper, six pounds a week, and four pounds a week more for my dinner at another house, without any drink.

"Yesterday, congress agreed to meet twice a day, so that we break up at one and meet at three o'clock. I told Mr. Shee my lodging was too dear and I did not like to lodge at one house and dine at another, half a mile off. He agreed to board me at twenty dollars a week including dinner, which is fifty shillings less than I had paid. I breakfasted with Mr. Wilson and Ross at Mrs. House's, she said her price was twenty dollars a week which I will accept of. . . . I am laying my account upon returning about the tenth of next month, to be able to attend Carlisle and York courts.

"Beef and mutton are half a crown, veal three shillings, and all kind of goods as dear as ever. . . . I put fifteen hundred pounds in the loan office, and have got about ninety pounds fees, and a promise of a hundred pounds fee more, these are the first fees I ever got in Philadelphia; my fees here must clear my teeth, and my pay in Congress go to you, dear, and the children. I believe that if you would consent to come here to live I could get into pretty good business in the law way, but it is a hazard and two thousand a year would, as times go, be not more than enough to live in any tolerable style here. York and Carlisle are sure for business though fees are not as high as here. . . . Poor Mrs. Shugart with Mr. Armor called upon me to assist in getting a pass from Congress for leave for her to go to New York to try and get her husband home. I much doubt her success, but got her the pass. Our prisoners there, whose friends cannot send them hard money, suffer greatly. I tried to get Tommy Armor a good post in the army but missed it; had he written me in time, I believe I might have had it for him.

"You, my dear, have been fatigued to death with the plantation affairs; I can only pity but not help you. . . . I have not time to finish, but you will have had nonsense enough, Your loving husband, whilest. James Smith."

Congressman Smith died in 1806 and his monument says that he was ninety-three years old. He was buried in York and his wife sleeps beside him.

Nancy Savage Taylor

One of the Revolutionary women, to whom history has done scant justice, was Mrs. Nancy

Savage who, in 1739, became the wife of George Taylor and was the mother of his two children.

The story of George Taylor is an interesting one. He was born in Ireland, in 1716; the son of a clergyman who gave him a good education and who wanted him to study medicine. This was distasteful to the lad and he ran away and shipped for America as a "redemptioner." That is, the shipmaster was given the right to sell the lad's services on this side to pay for his passage. At Philadelphia, Mr. Savage, lessee of the Durham iron works, a short distance below Easton, paid young Taylor's redemption money, and the boy bound himself to work a certain number of years to repay the debt. He was large for his age, strong and sturdy, and was set to work as "filler," shovelling coal into the furnace when in blast. Mr. Savage soon discovered that the lad was not bred to manual labour and also that he was educated far above his other workmen and was trustworthy and industrious, and transferred him to his business office. Taylor mastered the business in all its details and, after completing his indenture, remained with Mr. Savage until the latter's death in 1738. Mrs. Savage, who

was considerably younger than her husband and
had no children, knew little of the business which
Taylor continued to manage, and about a year
later he married the widow and became, at the
age of twenty-three, sole lessee of the iron works
where, a few years before, he had come as a
"redemptioner." He continued at Durham,
until 1764, accumulating a handsome property.
Then he removed to Northumberland County
where he purchased an estate on the Lehigh
River, built a large stone house, and started
another iron works.

Ten years later, Mr. Taylor returned to
Durham and in partnership with a man named
Galloway leased the furnace once more, and
began turning out stoves of his own designing,
and after 1775, vast amounts of shot and other
munitions of war. In 1764, he was elected to
the Provincial Assembly and thereafter was
active in public affairs until his death in 1781,
at his home in Easton where he and his wife
were buried.

Two children were born to the redemptioner
and his wife, one son and one daughter. The
son, James Taylor, who became a lawyer,
married Elizabeth, daughter of Lewis Gordon,

the first attorney of Northumberland county and died in 1772, leaving five children.[6] George Taylor's daughter died unmarried.

Rachael Bird Wilson

Rachael Bird, the youngest daughter of William Bird of Bucks County, Pennsylvania, proprietor of the fine country seat and iron works on the Schuylkill River, known as Birdsborough, became, in 1771 or 1772, the first wife of James Wilson. He was a young lawyer at the time, having been but recently admitted to the practice of law after completing his studies in the office of John Dickinson, one of the most celebrated barristers of his day. Wilson was a highly educated young Englishman who had come to this country in 1766, with letters of introduction to some of the most prominent men of New York and Philadelphia. After being admitted to the bar he practised for two or three years in Reading and Carlisle and in Annapolis, after which he took up his permanent residence in Philadelphia. Very early in his legal career, he became a strong adherent of the American cause, and during the remainder of his life much of his time and great abilities were devoted to public affairs, either in the State of his adoption or under the new national government. He died suddenly in 1798, in North Carolina, at Edenton, where he was presiding at a session of the federal court to which he had been appointed by President Washington. His wife, Rachael Bird, had died twelve years before, in 1786, leaving five children: Mary, who married Paschal Hollingsworth, of Philadelphia; William, who died at Kaskaskia in 1817; Bird, who held a judicial position in Pennsylvania and afterward became a clergyman in New York; James, who was a lieutenant in the army, resigned his commission and became a merchant and died at St. Domingo in 1808; Charles was first a midshipman in the navy and afterward in a mercantile business and died in Havana in 1800. The children whose decease is noted, died unmarried.

Judge Wilson married for his second wife, Hannah Gray, "an amiable young lady of Boston," second daughter of Ellis Gray, a merchant of that city. One child was born of this marriage, Henry, who died in infancy. Mrs. Wilson survived her husband and later married Dr. Thomas Bartlett of Boston and died in London in 1807.

Ann Lawler Ross

Ann Lawler, described in Harris's *History of Lancaster*, as "a lady of respectable family," was the only child of Mary Lawler, a widow of Lancaster, Pennsylvania, possessed of considerable property and who died in 1778. She was a handsome accomplished young woman, and her marriage to George Ross, August 14, 1751, was considered a highly advantageous union for both.[7] George Ross was born in Newcastle, Delaware, where his father who was twice married and had eleven children, all of whom became prominent members of society, was clergyman of the Episcopal Church. Catharine, eldest sister of George Ross, was the wife of Captain William Thompson, afterward a general of the Continental army; Gertrude, another sister, married Hon. George Read of Delaware, who afterward became one of the signers of the Declaration of Independence. A third sister, Mary, married Col. Mark Bird, of Birdsborough, a prominent Pennsylvanian and an active patriot. Still another became the wife of Col. Edward Biddle of Reading, speaker of the Pennsylvania Legislature and member of the first and second Continental Congresses. Two sisters, Margaret and Susannah, married prominent clergymen, and three brothers were each members of the learned professions.

George Ross was well educated by his father and afterward studied law with his brother, John Ross, one of the foremost practitioners of his day and a warm personal friend of Benjamin Franklin. Later he took up his residence in Lancaster. In 1768, he was elected a member of the Provincial Legislature and from that time, he was almost continuously in the public service until his death, July 14, 1779. His wife's death took place several years before this.

Three children were born to George and Ann Ross, George, James, and Mary. George Ross, Jr., the eldest, was a staunch patriot during the Revolution and was for some time Vice-President of the Supreme Executive Council of Pennsylvania. In 1791 he was commissioned by the Governor, Register and Recorder, which office he held for eighteen years.

James Ross, his brother, raised in 1775, the

first company in Lancaster County, in Colonel Thompson's regiment of which he was made captain, and marched to Cambridge. He rose to the rank of Lieutenant-Colonel of the Eighth Pennsylvania Regiment with which he fought at Long Island, Trenton, Germantown, Brandywine, and in other important engagements. Mary Ross married Joshua Scott, a noted civil engineer, and died in 1839.

Egle's *Notes and Queries* says of the Ross family: "Ann (Lawler) Ross was greatly celebrated for her beauty and her children were so remarkable in this respect as to attract general notice."

Gertrude Ross Read

Gertrude Ross Till, the young widow of Thomas Till, who in 1763 put aside her weeds to become the wife of George Read,[8] a prominent young lawyer of Newcastle, Delaware, was the daughter of Reverend George Ross, who was for more than half a century a clergyman of that town. Also, she was the sister of George Ross, afterward, like her husband, a signer of the Declaration of Independence and a half-sister of John Ross, an eminent legal practitioner at the Philadelphia bar.

She seems to have been admirably fitted
to be the life companion of the public-spirited
and patriotic young man she married. Read,
who after having received an excellent classical
education was admitted to the bar at the age
of nineteen, was a man of the highest principles.
As the eldest of his father's six children, he was
entitled, under existing Delaware laws, to two
fifths of his father's estate.   As soon as he came
of age, he made over all his rights in the estate
to the younger children on the plea that the
amount spent upon his education was all that
he could ask from the estate by right.   When the
contest between Great Britain and her Colonies
began in 1765, he held office under the Crown,
Attorney-General   for   the   "lower   counties"
in Delaware, but that did not prevent him from
entering actively into every measure to protect the
rights of the people.   From that time until
his death in 1798 he was always in the public
service, member of Congress, Judge of the Court
of Appeals, United States Senator, and Chief
Justice of Delaware.

Gertrude had been highly educated by her
father. Her understanding, naturally strong,
was carefully cultivated by him, beyond the

common lot of most girls of her days even in educated families. Moreover, it is said, "her person was beautiful, her manners elegant, and her piety exemplary."

"During the Revolution," says Sanderson, "she was almost constantly separated from her husband owing to his unremitting service to his country. She herself suffered considerable hardship, being often compelled to fly from her home at a moment's notice and this encumbered with an infant family. But she was never dejected or complaining; on the contrary, encouraged her husband in every possible way, not only by word but by the cheerful manner in which she bore the hardships and burdens which fell to her lot."

Mrs. Read's life during the Revolution was a troubled one. The enemy was almost constantly on the maritime border of Delaware and kept the little Province in a continuous state of alarm by predatory incursions. The British army at different periods occupied parts of its territory or went across it making frequent changes of habitation necessary.

While in Congress, Mr. Read wrote as freely to his wife about public affairs as about their domestic concerns, and always in the same spirit of delightful comradeship. In 1774, two days before the adjournment of Congress he wrote:

"MY DEAR G——, I am still uncertain as to the time of my return home. As I expected it, the New England men declined doing any business on Sunday and though we sat until four o'clock this afternoon, I am well persuaded that our business can by no means be left until Wednesday evening and even then very doubtful, so that I have no prospect in being with you till Thursday evening. Five of the Virginia men are gone. The two remaining ones have power to act in their stead. The two objects before us, and what we are to go through to-morrow, are an address to the king and one to the people of Canada. This last was recommitted this evening in order to be remodelled. Your brother George (the Signer) came to Congress this afternoon. All your friends are well. No news but the burning of the vessel and tea at Annapolis (the *Peggy Stewart*) which I take for granted you will have heard before this comes to hand. We are all well at my lodgings, and send their love to you."

Another letter, written in 1776, is as follows:

"MY DEAR G——, I have this morning wrote to Katy Thompson (his sister wife of General Thompson) proposing to her to send her oldest son George, to Philadelphia, to the college, where Ned Biddle (another brother-in-law) will provide him with board and lodging, and that she should send her second son to Wilmington, where you will do the like for him. I presume that you will approve of this last.

"The Province ship left the town yesterday, being hurried off in consequence of intelligence that the *Roebuck*, man-of-war, was ashore near the cape. A ship fitted out by Congress and called the *Reprisal*, is ordered down also with several of the gondolas, but a report prevailed last evening that the *Roebuck* had got off. Little else has been talked of since the Sunday noon that the news came. I flatter myself that I shall see you on Saturday next. Last Saturday the Congress sat, and I could not be absent. I saw Mr. Bedford last evening: he had a little gout in both feet, attended with a fever: of this last he most complained, but it is

gone off.   This day is their election for additional
members of Assembly.   Great strife is expected.
Their fixed candidates are not known.   One
side talk of Thomas Willing, Andrew Allen,
Alexander Wilcox, and Samuel Howell, against
independence: the other, Daniel Robertdeau,
George Clymer, Mark Kuhl, and the fourth I
do not recollect: but it is thought that other
persons will be put up.   My love to our little
ones, and compliments to all acquaintances."

Mrs. Read was noted for her fondness and
taste for horticulture and was very fond of the
profusion of flowers, especially tulips, which
grew in the extensive garden of the old-fashioned
mansion, in Newcastle.   There she spent
most of her life except for the short periods,
during the Revolution, when she was forced,
for safety, to take her family to Wilmington
or Philadelphia.

There were five children born to Gertrude and
George Read, four sons and one daughter.
John Read, the first born, died in infancy;
George Read, Jr., the next son, born in 1765,
was U. S. District Attorney for Delaware for
thirty years, receiving his first appointment

from Washington. He married his cousin, Mary Thompson. William, born 1767, married Anne McCall. He was Consul-General for Naples at Philadelphia for many years; John, born 1769, married Martha, eldest daughter of Samuel Meredith, brother-in-law of George Clymer, the signer. He was a prominent member of the Philadelphia bar and Judge of the Superior Court of Pennsylvania. His son, Gen. John M. Read was U. S. Consul-General at Paris. Mary Howell, the signer's only daughter, married Matthew Pearce of Maryland.

Mary Borden McKean

Mary Borden, who in 1763,[9] became the first wife of Thomas McKean, was the eldest daughter of Thomas Borden of Bordentown, New Jersey, a wealthy and public-spirited citizen, who was later to become an active patriot during the war of the Revolution. Mary Borden and her younger sister, Ann, were said to be the handsomest girls in New Jersey. Ann afterward married Francis Hopkinson, who like his brother-in-law, Thomas McKean, became a signer of the Declaration of Independence.

Thomas McKean was the son of well-to-do

Irish-American parents who had settled in Chester County. He was educated in the celebrated school of Rev. Francis Allison of Philadelphia, after which he studied law in the office of David Finney, a prominent attorney of Newcastle, Delaware, where before he was twenty years old he was appointed deputy prothonotary and register of the probate court of Newcastle County. The highly active public life of Mr. McKean, from his admission to the bar in the early fifties, almost to the day of his death, in 1817, was not exceeded in usefulness by any other public man of his day. During that period he held at one time or another most of the high official positions in Pennsylvania and Delaware, sometimes filling several offices at the same time.[10] In 1777, for instance, he represented Delaware in the Continental Congress, was chief justice of Pennsylvania, and president of Congress. The chief justiceship he held for twenty-two years, after which he was governor of Pennsylvania for nine years.

Mary Borden lived only ten years after her marriage, not long enough to enjoy much of the success that came to her husband later in life, but long enough to bear him six children, who were as follows:

Joseph Borden, born 1764; Robert, born 1765; Elizabeth, born 1767, married Andrew Pettit; Letitia, born 1769, married George Buchanan; Mary, born 1771, died in childhood; Anne, born in 1773, married Andrew Buchanan.

Sarah Armitage of Newcastle became the second wife of Thomas McKean, September 2, 1774. Their first child, a son, died in infancy; Sarah, the second, born July 8, 1777, became the Marchioness de Casa Yrujo; Sophia Dorothea, born 1783,[11] and Maria Louisa, born 1785, died unmarried.

Anne Baldwin Chase

Anne Baldwin of Annapolis, Md., was the first wife of Samuel Chase to whom she was married in 1762. He was twenty-one years old at the time, and had just completed his legal studies, which had been prosecuted under the direction of John Hammond and John Hall, two prominent attorneys of Annapolis. He established a lucrative practice in that city and early began taking the intelligent and active interest in public affairs that was later to make him so uncompromising a patriot and so valuable a member of the Continental Congress. William Paca was a fellow student with Samuel Chase in the office of Hammond & Hall and there began a friendship which was never broken. The two young men became members of the Provincial Legislature the same year and together were sent to the Continental Congress.

The young wife was not permitted to enjoy the honours that were to come to her husband, for she died during the early days of the Revolution, leaving six children, two sons and four daughters.[12]

In March, 1783, Mr. Chase went to England on legal business and there met and married Miss Hannah Kilty Giles, of London, who bore him two daughters. The eldest, Eliza, married Dr. Skipwith Coale, of London and the second daughter, Hannah, married William Barney, Esq., son of Commodore Barney of the Revolutionary navy.

In 1786, Judge Chase removed to Baltimore, where his warm personal friend, Col. John E. Howard, son-in-law of Benjamin Chew, and afterward U. S. Senator, presented him with a square in a newly laid out part of the city of

Baltimore, on condition that he would take up his residence there. Judge Chase was not a man of means, but the rapid rise in value of the property which comprised many city lots, aside from what the Judge reserved for his own spacious mansion, afforded him a competence. Here he died in 1811.

Mary Chew Paca

Mary Chew, who married William Paca in 1761, was the daughter of Samuel Chew and Henrietta Lloyd, and a direct descendant of John Chew, who arrived at Jamestown in 1622, with three servants, on the ship *Charitie*. Of the young woman we have but little record except that she was the favourite granddaughter of Samuel Chew, head of one of the oldest and most prominent Colonial families. In his *Historic Families of America*, Spooner says of the Chews: "They belong to that remarkable group of families which, founded in the Southern Colonies by ancestors of excellent birth and breeding, assumed at once a position of social and public consequence, and subsequent generations, by the merits and character of their members, as well as by influential alliances, steadily maintained and strengthened their original prestige."

William Paca, at the time of his marriage, was a young lawyer who had just reached his majority and had been elected a member of the Provincial Assembly. His young wife did not long survive to enjoy the successes and triumphs that came to her husband during his honoured public career, in which he was member of Congress, Justice of the Supreme Court of his native State, and finally its Governor. She died in the opening year of the Revolution. She was the mother of five children, only one of whom survived, according to Sanderson.[13]   This was a son, John P. Paca, who afterward married Juliana, daughter of Richard and Mary Tighlman.

In 1777, Mr. Paca married a second wife, Miss Anne Harrison, a highly respected young woman of Philadelphia, who died three years later, leaving one child, which did not long survive her. Governor Paca died in 1799 at his ancestral home, Wye Hall, Harford County.

Margaret Brown Stone

Margaret Brown, who in 1746 married Thomas Stone, afterward delegate to the Continental

Congress from Maryland and signer of the Declaration of Independence, was the youngest daughter of Dr. Gustavus Brown of Port Tobacco, Charles County, Maryland. Of her family we have the following from Hayden's *Virginia Genealogies:*

"Gustavus Brown, M.D., of 'Rich Hill,' Charles County, Md., and Laird of Mainside and House Byers, Roxburgh, Scotland, born Dalkeith, Scotland, Apr. 10, 1689; died of apoplexy, 'Rich Hill,' Apr., 1762; married, 1st, 1710, Frances Fowke, daughter of Col. Gerard and Sarah (Burdette) Fowke, of Charles County; he married, 2d, Margaret (Black) Boyd, widow of an Irish gentleman and merchant of Port Tobacco.

"When a youth of 19 he became a surgeon's mate, or surgeon, on one of the royal or King's ships that came to the Colony in the Chesapeake Bay. In 1708, while his ship lay at anchor he went ashore, but before he could return a severe storm arose, which made it necessary for the ship to weigh anchor and put to sea. The young man was left with nothing but the clothes on his back. He quickly made himself known, and informed the planters of his willingness to serve them if he could be provided with instruments and medicines, leaving them to judge if he were worthy of their confidence. He began the practice of medicine at Nansemond, Md. He soon gained respect and succeeded beyond expectations. He married into a wealthy family, made a large fortune, and wishing to lay his bones in his own loved Scotland, returned there with his family, and became possessed, by purchase it is believed, possibly by inheritance, of the lands he disposed of by will. His wife became dissatisfied with Scotland and he returned in 1734 to Maryland, where he had years before purchased the seat of Col. Lomax, called 'Rich Hill,' four miles from Port Tobacco, Charles Co."—(TONER)

In the family Bible of Dr. Brown, which is still in possession of his descendants, is the following: "This Bible originally belonged to Jane Mitchelson, my mother, who was daughter to George Mitchelson, grandson of the house of Middleton, near Dalkeith, and Isabel Elfston, daughter of Solomon, seven miles to the west of Edinburgh. I came into Maryland in May, anno 1708, and anno 1710, married Frances Fowke the daughter of Mr. Gerard Fowke in Nanjemy—of which marriage the following children were born, viz.: Gustavus Brown (or Broun as called in Scotland) was born December 7, 1711. My daughter Frances Brown was born July 29, 1713. My daughter Sarah Brown was born August 29, 1715. My daugh'r Mary Brown was born Dec. 8, 1717. My daugh'r Christina was born Aug. 29, 1720. My second son Gustavus was born September the 5th, in 1722, and died the 8th day of his age, as did my eldest son in the 9th month. My daughter Elizabeth Brown was born in Oct. 5th, 1723. My son Rich'd Brown was born Dec. 2d, 1725. My fourth son Gustavus was born May 30, 1727, and died the 9th June following. Jane was born June 1st, 1728."

Then was added in a different hand, as follows: "The following memorandum made by Gustavus Rich'd Brown, last son of the above named Gustavus Brown: a daughter Ann was born by the first marriage, not mentioned by my father. After the death of his first wife my father married Margaret Boid from whom I descended. I was born on the 17th of Oct., 1747. A sister, Margaret, was born about two years after and married Thomas Stone, Esquire."

Miss Margaret is described, at the time of her

marriage in 1762, as being "adorned with elevated talents and blest with piety, and every female virtue." When they were wed, Thomas Stone received with his bride £1000 sterling and with this money he purchased the plantation, "Havre de Venture," situated about two miles from Port Tobacco, and there he resided during the Revolution. Mrs. Stone died in 1787 under the following circumstances as told by R. M. Conway in *Virginia Genealogies:* "In 1785, when Congress adjourned, he (Thomas Stone) retired from public life, having served his State in the Legislature as well as Congress, and engaged in the duties of his profession, being often employed in cases of great importance. In 1787 his wife, to whom he was tenderly attached, was innoculated with small pox (the only method then known to modify the disease and escape its worst ills), and was unskilfully treated. After suffering untold misery, through which Mr. Stone watched with the utmost devotion and solicitude for weeks, death ensued. This occurrence, under such terrible circumstances, threw a deep melancholy over the spirits of Mr. Stone, and his health steadily declined. He died October 5, 1787, aged forty-five years. He was a lineal descendant of William Stone, Governor of Maryland during the time of Oliver Cromwell. His brother, John Hoskins Stone, was Governor of the State, 1794–97."

Three children were born to Mary Brown and Thomas Stone: Frederick, who died while pursuing his law studies in Philadelphia, during the yellow-fever epidemic of 1793; Mildred, born in 1771, who married Travers Daniels of "Cleremont," Stafford County, Va.; and Margaret Eleanor who became the second wife of John Moncure Daniel of the "Crows Nest," Stafford County, Va.

Mary Darnell Carroll

Mary Darnell, daughter of Col. Henry Darnell and Rachel Brooke, of Prince George County, Maryland, was married to her distant cousin, the knightly Charles Carroll of Carrollton, in June, 1768, and the *Maryland Gazette* of that date makes this announcement:

"On Sunday evening at his Father's house in this city (Annapolis), Charles Carroll, jr., Esq., was married to Miss Mary Darnell, an agreeable young Lady endowed with every accomplishment necessary to render the connubial state happy."

Charles Carroll's own estimate of the young lady at the time may be learned from a letter that he wrote to a personal friend, August 13, 1767, which has been preserved:

"DEAR JENNINGS: Perhaps before you receive this I shall be married. I have been so successful as to gain the affections of a young lady endowed with every quality to make me happy in the married state, virtue, good sense, good temper. These too receive no small lustre from her person which the partiality of a lover does not represent to me more agreeable than what it really is. She really is a sweet-tempered, charming girl—a little too young for me, I confess, especially as I am of weak and puny constitution. . . ."

In the following January, Carroll wrote to another friend, as follows:

"MY DEAR GRAVES:
I hope you received my last letter of the 7th of November. By that you will learn that my marriage with Miss Darnell was put off till the next spring, in order to obtain an Act of Assembly. . . . Thus you see if the settlement cannot

be securely made without an act to give it legal force, I may wait two years longer, that is, till the young lady comes of age. She will be nineteen years old the 19th of next March. . . . The young lady to whom I am to give my hand and who already has my heart, altho' blessed in every good quality, has not been favoured by fortune in respect to money. . . ."

The matter seems to have been settled satisfactorily, however, for on Saturday, June 4th, 1768, the marriage contract was drawn and styled "an Indenture between Charles Carroll of Carrollton, of the first part, Henry Darnell, jr., of the second part, Rachel Darnell, wife of said Henry, of the third part, Mary Darnell, daughter of said Henry and Rachel, of the fourth part, and Robert Darnell, uncle of said Mary, of the fifth part." Their marriage took place the following day.

Six daughters and one son were born to the Carrolls, but four of the daughters died in infancy or early childhood. The other children were as follows: Mary, born in 1770, married Richard Caton, son of Joseph Caton of Liverpool, England; Charles, afterward known as Charles Carrollton of Homewood, born in 1775, married Harriet Chew, daughter of Benjamin Chew of Philadelphia; and Catharine, born in 1778, married Robert Goodloe Harper.

Mrs. Carroll died in 1782 in the thirty-fifth year of her age. The writer of the Carroll sketches in *Appleton's Journal* of September, 1874, tells the story of her death as follows: "The death of Mrs. Carroll was very sad. She was devotedly attached to her grandfather [father-in-law]. One day he was standing on the large porch of his house in Annapolis, watching a ship come into the harbour. He stepped back too far and was picked up dead. Mrs. Carroll, his child by marriage and his constant companion, never recovered from the shock, nor left her room afterward until death."

A New York writer of half a century ago paid this tribute to Carroll of Carrollton, and his family:

"The Senator from Maryland, Charles Carroll, was in many respects one of the most remarkable men in a remarkable body. His family had been settled in Maryland since the days of James II and became gradually possessors of enormous estates. Educated abroad with the utmost care, Mr. Carroll's long foreign

Mrs. Charles Carroll (Harriet Chew).
From a picture by John Trumbull.

residence, at a time when his mind was most open to receive permanent impressions, had not operated to alienate his love of country, and he returned to it more devoted than before. No one had more to lose in the desperate venture of rebellion and revolution than himself, yet none was more unflinching in his action.

"Thus it happened that no man was more respected and beloved and though his fortune had given him immense possessions, to no one were they less grudged by the envious and jealous vulgar. Lord Brougham in commenting on this remarkable character in the *Edinburgh Review* essays, speaks of him as a scholar of extraordinary accomplishments, whom few if any of the speakers of the new world approached in his nearness to the model of the refined oratory practised in the parent state. During the second session of Congress in New York, he was accompanied by several members of his family, who were destined to become connected with the most dignified representatives of the English nobility. His daughter, Polly Carroll, had, a few years before in Baltimore, become the wife of Mr. Richard Caton, an English gentleman. As early as 1809, two of the Miss Catons had become reigning belles; one of them, Mrs. Robert Patterson, while in Europe attracted the admiration of Sir Arthur Wellesley, the future hero of Waterloo, to such an extent that he followed her all over Europe, thereby causing much scandal. Mrs. Patterson afterward became a widow, and captivated Sir Arthur's elder brother, the Marquis of Wellesley, who offered her the coronet of a Marchioness. Another sister was the Duchess of Leeds, and a second married Baron Stafford.

"Mrs. Charles Carroll, jr., was one of the few ladies of official rank in the times of Washington. Her father, Benjamin Chew, was Chief Justice of Pennsylvania, and his great wealth, princely style of living, and superior abilities gave him an exalted standing alike in public and social affairs. Both Mrs. Carroll (Mrs. Charles, jr.) and her sister Mrs. Henry Phillips were great favourites with Gen. Washington and much in his society as young ladies; a third sister became the wife of Col. John Eager Howard, who was ultimately one of the Senators from Maryland."

Charles Carroll never married again, but lived until 1832, when he died in Baltimore at the honoured age of ninety-five years, the last of the signers of the Declaration of Independence.[14]

Anne Lewis Wythe

Anne Lewis, who in 1756 became the wife of George Wythe, was the eldest of ten children born to Zachary and Mary Waller Lewis of Spottsylvania County, Virginia. She was born August 30. 1726, the same year as the young law student who led her to the altar thirty years later.

Her father was an eminent Colonial lawyer who had built up a fortune from his practice and owned a large landed estate. There is a road in Spottsylvania County which to this day bears the name "The Lawyers' Road," because of the fact that it was travelled so frequently by Mr. Lewis and his son, John Lewis, going to and from the court house in the adjoining county of Orange.

Of George Wythe, Hayden's *Virginia Genealogies* says: "Chancellor Wythe was the son of Mr. Wythe, who owned a good estate on Black River, and died leaving a widow and three children. His mother was one of five daughters of Mr. Keith, a Quaker and author of a work on

mathematics, who came from England to Hampden in 1690." Mr. Wythe was educated by his
mother, and studied law with his uncle-in-law,
Mr. Dewey of Prince George County. His
mother died in 1746. Then came a lapse in the
life of the young man; left an orphan before he
was twenty-one, with an ample fortune, he gave
way to what an apologetic biographer has called
"the seductions of pleasure," laid study aside,
and devoted several years to amusement and
dissipation. In the course of a few years, however, he seems to have come to sober reflection,
for at the age of about thirty, he withdrew himself from his gay associates, relinquished his
levities, and returned to his studies with a zeal
and application which prepared him for the distinguished honour and usefulness to which he
afterward attained.

It was Miss Anne Lewis who seems to have
brought Mr. Wythe to "sober reflection." He
was married in 1756 and soon afterward was
admitted to practice at Williamsburg. In 1758
he was elected a member of the House of Burgesses. That was the beginning of the splendid
career of George Wythe, who became a patriot
of the Revolution with such confrères as the

Lees, Harrison, Peyton Randolph, Col. Bland, and Patrick Henry, a professor of law in the College of William and Mary, during which he had the honour of having been law instructor to two young men who afterward became Presidents of the United States and one destined for the highest place on the Supreme Bench. From the chair of law in William and Mary, Judge Wythe became Chancellor of Virginia.

Mrs. Wythe died some time in the later sixties, leaving no children. A few years afterward, Mr. Wythe was married to Elizabeth Talliaferro, of "Powhatan," near Williamsburg, but no children were born of the union. Chancellor Wythe died in 1806 and it was generally believed that he was poisoned. George Wythe Sweeney, a grandson of his sister, was tried for the murder but was acquitted. Before his death, Mr. Wythe gave freedom to all his slaves and made provision for their support until they should be able to care for themselves.

Anne Aylett Lee

Anne Aylett, the first wife of Richard Henry Lee, one of Virginia's most eminent and patriotic sons, came of a family as wealthy and prominent

as the Lees. In the *Historic Families of Virginia*
there is this note: "It is claimed that the Ayletts
are descended from a companion of the Con-
queror whose sons received grants in Cornwall.
In 1657, Captain John Aylett came to Virginia
and had a son William whose daughters intermarried with prominent families."

It would be interesting to know more of the
inner life and personality of Anne Aylett, and the
other notable women who shine in the reflected
light of husbands and fathers, to whom it was
given to fashion state policies and fight battles.
But such information has come down to us only
in isolated and fragmentary instances. Old Virginia differed materially from other provinces
and indeed from all other countries. Probably
in no other country were the women, generally, so
protected and sheltered as in the Old Dominion.
There were no large cities, and comparatively
little town life. Hospitality, not only as a virtue
but as a fine art, was exercised to an extent
equalled in no other Colony and rarely if ever
in any other country. The old families, with
their large estates, numerous house and field
servants, their wealth and culture, visited and
intermarried among themselves until the entire

commonwealth was like one big family. The
estates scattered over vast stretches of country,
sometimes miles apart, were not open to the
depredations of the enemy as were those of the
more thickly populated coast countries of Maryland and the Carolinas or the northern Colonies,
and when the men were called from home to the
council chamber or camp and field, the women
were not left unprotected as were those of South
Carolina, New Jersey, Long Island, or Connecticut, where for months at a time the country was
overrun with British troops, Hessians, and Tories. Consequently, if we find but little to tell,
in many instances, but family genealogy, it is not
because these women were less patriotic or loyal
to the cause of independence than their sisters of
less favoured localities. The steadfast patriotism of the husbands and fathers was a splendid
tribute to the loyal support and self-sacrifice of
the women.

It was about a century after the coming of
John Aylett to the Province of Virginia, that
Anne Aylett was married to Richard Henry, the
fifth son of Thomas and Hannah Ludwell Lee of
Stratford House, Westmoreland County.[15] She
was a cousin of Col. William Aylett, of "Fair-

field," King William County, and one of the
leading citizens of Virginia of his day. Anne Aylett's sister Mary married Richard Henry Lee's
brother, Thomas Ludwell Lee. A writer in the
William and Mary Quarterly says of the Aylett
family: "Col. Aylett was born about 1743. He
married, 1776, Mary Macon the daughter of Col.
Augustine Macon of 'Chelsea'. . . . Col. Aylett
was on intimate terms with General Washington.
When he visited headquarters, he is said by
Charles Campbell, the Virginia historian, to have
invariably slept in the General's tent. He and
Washington had been members of the House
of Burgesses at the same time. Col. Aylett's
mother and Mrs. Washington were first cousins.
Col. Aylett's brother, John, married a sister of
Mrs. Washington's. Elizabeth Macon, sister of
Mrs. Aylett, was married to Mrs. Washington's
brother Bartholomew Dandridge. Mrs. Washington's great-grandfather, Gideon Macon, was
Mrs. Aylett's grandfather. 'Fairfield,' Col. Aylett's home, being on the direct road between Mt.
Vernon, 'The White House' (Mrs. Washington's home when she married the second time)
and Williamsburg, the Washingtons generally
spent several days with their Aylett relations,

both going from and returning home. This was also the custom of Thomas Ludwell Lee and Richard Henry Lee, who married respectively Mary Aylett and Anne Alyett, first cousins of William Aylett. Augustine Washington, General Washington's brother, married Anne Aylett, another first cousin of Col. Aylett."

Children were born to Anne Aylett Lee as follows: Thomas, born October 20, 1758, lived at "Park Gate," Prince William County, won fame as a lawyer, married, first, Mildred, daughter of Augustine and Hannah Bushrod Washington, second, married Eliza Ashton Brent. Ludwell Lee, born 1760, served on the staff of General La Fayette, married his cousin Flora, daughter of Philip Ludwell and Elizabeth Steptoe Lee. Mary Lee, born 1764, married Colonel William Augustine Washington, son of Augustine and Anne Aylett Washington and nephew to the General. Hannah Lee, born about 1766, married Corbin Washington, son of John Augustine and Hannah Bushrod Washington (brother of the wife of her brother, Thomas Lee).

Anne Aylett Lee died in 1767, her thirty-fifth year, and two years later Mr. Lee married as his second wife Mrs. Anne Gaskins Pincard, daughter of Thomas Gaskins of Westmoreland County, and a sister of Colonel Thomas Gaskins, Jr., a distinguished officer of the Revolution. The children born of this union were: Anne Lee, born 1770, married her cousin, Charles Lee; Henrietta, born 1773, married Richard Lee Turberville; Sarah, born 1775, married her cousin, Edmund Jennings Lee, of Alexandria; and two sons, Cassius who died in boyhood and Francis Lightfoot. Mrs. Lee survived her husband, who died in 1794, but the date of her death is not given.

Martha Wayles Jefferson

Martha Skelton, daughter of John Wayles of "The Forest," in Charles City County, Virginia, was a young and beautiful widow when she was married to Thomas Jefferson, January 1, 1772. Her first husband, Bathurst Skelton, had died four years before, her only child had died in infancy, and she was living with her father at "The Forest." A pen picture of her at the time of her second marriage is given by Randall, in his *Life of Jefferson*. "Mrs. Skelton," he says, "was remarkable for her beauty, her accomplishments, and her solid merit. In person she was a little above medium height, slightly but

Martha Jefferson.
From the picture by T. Sully.

exquisitely formed. Her complexion was brilliant—her large expressive eyes of the richest
tinge of auburn. She walked, rode, and danced
with admirable grace and spirits; sang and
played the harpsichord and spinet with uncommon skill. The more solid parts of her education had not been overlooked."

Happily the biographer of Thomas Jefferson,
unlike most of those who have lent their pens to
perpetuate the memories of the Fathers of the
Republic, has not confined his observations entirely to the political side of his life, but has given
us delightful glimpses into the domestic. "She
was," he continues, "well read and intelligent,
conversed agreeably, possessed excellent sense,
and a lively play of fancy, and had a frank, warm-
hearted, and somewhat impulsive disposition."

Mrs. Jefferson was twenty-three years old at
the time of her second marriage, and her husband
was three years her senior. After graduating at
William and Mary College, he had studied law
under George Wythe and was enjoying a prosperous practice. After the wedding festivities
at "The Forest," Mrs. Jefferson and her husband set out for his home, Monticello, meeting
some unlooked-for adventures on the way. A

manuscript of Mrs. Randolph, their eldest daughter, and furnished to the biographer by her granddaughter, says: "They left 'The Forest' after a fall of snow, light then, but increasing in depth as they advanced up the country. They were finally obliged to quit the carriage and proceed on horseback. Having stopped for a short time at Blenheim (the residence of Col. Carter) where an overseer only resided, they left it at sunset to pursue their way through a mountain track, rather than a road, in which the snow lay from eighteen inches to two feet deep, having eight miles to go before reaching Monticello. They arrived late at night, the fires all out and the servants retired to their own houses for the night. The horrible dreariness of such a house at the end of such a journey, I have often heard both of them relate. Part of a bottle of wine found on a shelf behind some books had to serve them for both fire and supper."

There followed nine years of domestic happiness, mingled with the anxiety occasioned by the times, for both Mrs. Jefferson and her husband— nine years in which five little ones came to gladden their home and in which the husband had served his country and his State in ways that have left his name imperishable. Then came a time when Mrs. Jefferson began to show unmistakable signs of the decline that was to bring her to an untimely grave. Mr. Jefferson refused an important mission to Europe in order not to be separated from her, but was almost immediately called to the Executive chair of his native State. Several attempts had been made by the British to make him a prisoner. In November, 1779, Mrs. Jefferson's fifth child was born, and two months later she fled with it in her arms as Arnold approached Richmond. "The British General Tarleton sent troops to capture Governor Jefferson, who was occupied in securing his most important papers. While thus engaged, his wife and children were sent in a carriage to Colonel Coles, fourteen miles distant. Monticello was captured and the house searched, though not sacked, by the enemy. Many of the negroes were taken and but five ever returned. The farm was stripped of valuable horses and many thousand dollars' worth of tobacco and grain."

In April the loss of her infant, together with constant anxiety for the safety of her husband, shattered the remaining strength of Mrs.

Jefferson. Her last child was born in May, 1782, and she never rallied, but died early in September. Her eldest daughter, Mrs. Randolph, many years afterward, recorded her recollection of the sad event: "He [her father] nursed my poor mother in turn with Aunt Carr and her own sister, sitting up with her and administering medicines and drink to the last. For four months that she lingered, he was never out of calling; when not at her bedside, he was writing in a small room which opened immediately at the head of her bed. A moment before the closing scene, he was led from the room almost in a state of insensibility by his sister, Mrs. Carr, who with great difficulty got him into his library, where he fainted and remained so long insensible that we thought he would never revive. The scene that followed I did not witness, but the violence of his emotion, when almost by stealth I entered his room at night, to this day I dare not trust myself to describe. He kept his room three weeks and I was never a moment from his side. He walked almost incessantly, night and day, only lying down occasionally, when nature was completely exhausted, on a pallet that had been brought in during his long fainting fits. My aunts remained almost constantly with him for some weeks. I do not know how many. When at last he left his room, he rode out and from that time he was incessantly on horseback rambling about the mountain in the least frequented roads and just as often through the woods. In those melancholy rambles, I was his companion, a solitary witness to many a violent outburst of grief, the remembrance of which has consecrated particular stones of that lost home beyond the power of time to obliterate."

Mrs. Jefferson was survived by three daughters: Martha, who married Thomas Mann Randolph, Jr., who had been a ward of her father; Mary, born in 1778, who married John Wayles Eppes; and Lucy Elizabeth, who died in childhood.[16]

Elizabeth Bassett Harrison

Elizabeth Bassett, who became the wife of Benjamin Harrison, afterward signer of the Declaration of Independence, was the daughter of Colonel William Bassett, and was born about 1741 or 1742 on his estate "Eltham," in Kent County. Not much has come down to us of her girlhood or her personality, even the exact date of her birth or her marriage being un-known.

She was famed for her beauty and her accomplishments as a girl, as she was in later life for her exemplary piety and benevolence, but that is about all Mr. Harrison's biographers have seen fit to tell. But as she was related to many of the most noted families of Virginia and her father a man of wealth and social prominence, we may presume that she was a most gracious hostess, and from the high character of her sons and daughters, we know that she was a mother of the true Old Dominion type.

Benjamin Harrison, father of the signer, was one of the largest landholders and one of the most prominent men of Virginia, and his wife was Anne Carter, daughter of Robert Carter, "King Carter of Corotoman," Lancaster County, Speaker of the House of Burgesses and Rector of William and Mary College. Benjamin Harrison, the elder, was killed by a stroke of lightning at Berkeley, and his son Benjamin, the eldest of six brothers, who had not yet attained his majority, became the head of the house and owner of the estate, and it was to Berkeley that he brought his bride, and there they lived during the remainder of their lives, she surviving him about a year. He died in 1791, after having filled with honours many important offices of trust, from Speaker of the House of Burgesses to the Executive chair of his native State and several terms in Congress, of which Peyton Randolph, who was married to one of his sisters, was the first President.

A number of children were born to Elizabeth Harrison and her husband, seven of whom survived infancy, three sons and four daughters. Of the sons, Benjamin, the eldest, was sent to Philadelphia and placed in the counting room of Robert Morris, after which he visited Europe, where he formed several important commercial connections. During the Revolution he was Paymaster General of the Southern Department. After peace was restored, he established himself as a merchant in Richmond, and there acquired a large fortune. A great deal of this he sacrificed to aid his early friend Robert Morris when the latter became involved. He was married twice, first to Anne Mercer, and second, to Susannah Randolph.

Carter Bassett, the second son, was graduated from William and Mary College, became a lawyer and served in the State Legislature and was a member of Congress in 1793. He married Mary Howell Allen.

The third son, William Henry Harrison, was educated at Hampden Sidney College in Virginia, went into the army, and in 1841 became President of the United States. He married Anne Symmes and they were the great-grandparents of the late President Benjamin Harrison.

Of the daughters of Elizabeth Bassett Harrison, Lucy the eldest married her cousin, Peyton Randolph, nephew of Peyton Randolph, the first President of Congress. Anne, the second daughter, married David O. Copeland, and Sarah married John Wing of Weynoke.[17]

Lucy Grymes Nelson

Lucy Grymes, daughter of Philip Grymes, Esq., of Middlesex County, Va., and his wife Mary, daughter of Sir John Randolph of Williamsburg, was a beautiful girl of refined manners and retiring nature when she was married, Aug. 29, 1762, to Thomas Nelson, Jr., of York. It was a union notable for its fitness. The young woman was slightly the junior of her husband. She was the daughter of a wealthy

planter, prominent in the business and political
life of the Province and noted for his public
spirit and hospitality, and through her mother
she was related to many of the notable families
of Virginia.

Young Nelson was a descendant of Thomas
Nelson, who had come to Virginia about the
beginning of the century, founded the town of
York, according to Bishop Meade's *Recollec-
tions*, established a mercantile business and
grown wealthy. His family had married into
other families of York County and established
strong connections. The young man had been
educated abroad at Trinity College, returning a
year before his marriage. He settled in York
and is said to have "lived in much style and
hospitality." Soon after his marriage he was
elected to the House of Burgesses, and from that
time until his untimely death at the age of fifty
years he was almost continuously in the public
service. He was first a colonel of militia, then
brigadier-general of the State troops, member of
Congress, and finally Governor. He was an ardent
and active patriot, sacrificing most of his fortune
in aid of the cause. Virginia achieved a glorious
record for her sons in that struggle and not the

least of them was Governor Thomas Nelson. And always, we are told, he was loyally supported by his wife, who had her own burdens to bear by reason of the prominent part he played.

Eleven children were born to them, as follows: William, the eldest son, born 1763, married Sally Burwell, eldest daughter of Governor John Page. Thomas Nelson, Jr., born 1764, married Frances, a daughter of Governor John Page. Philip Nelson, the third son, born 1766, married Sarah N. Burwell of Clarke County. Francis Nelson, born 1767, married Lucy, youngest daughter of Hon. John Page of Gloucester (now Matthews) County. Hon. Hugh Nelson, born 1768, married Eliza, daughter of Francis Kinlock of South Carolina. Elizabeth Nelson, born 1770, married Mann Page, eldest son of Governor John Page. Mary Nelson, born 1774, married Robert Carter of Shirley. Lucy Nelson, born 1777, married Carter Page, of Cumberland County, and was his second wife. Robert Nelson, born 1778, married Judith Carter, youngest daughter of Governor John Page. He was called "Chancellor Nelson" from having been Chancellor of William and Mary College, where he was for many years Professor of Law. Susannah Nelson, born 1780, married Francis Page of Hanover County, son of Governor John Page. Judith Nelson, born 1783, married Captain Thomas Nelson of Hanover County. Thus it will be seen that five of the children of Elizabeth and Thomas Nelson married five of the children of Governor John Page, and two of them were married to children of Hon. John Page of Gloucester County.[18]

Mistress Nelson survived her husband many years, living to be eighty years old and died, "leaving" as Bishop Meade has said, "twenty dollars to her minister and freedom to her servant, the only one she had."

When Thomas Nelson died January 4, 1789, just after completing his fiftieth year, writes his biographer, "he descended into the grave honoured and beloved, and alas! of his once vast estates, that honour and love was almost all that he left behind him. He had spent a princely fortune in his Country's service; his horses had been taken from the plough and sent to drag the munitions of war; his granaries had been thrown open to a starving soldiery and his ample purse had been drained to its last dollar, when the credit of Virginia could not bring a sixpence into her treasury. Yet it was the widow of this man who, beyond eighty years of age, blind, infirm, and poor, had yet to learn whether republics can be grateful."

Rebecca Tayloe Lee

Rebecca Tayloe, who at the age of nineteen years became the wife of Francis Lightfoot Lee in May, 1769, was the second of the eleven children born to Colonel John and Rebecca Plater Tayloe, of "Mt. Airy," Richmond County, one of the most noted houses of Virginia. She was a highly accomplished and popular young woman and an estimable wife to Mr. Lee, who was the fourth son of Thomas Lee and younger brother to Richard Henry Lee. His father died and left him a fortune while he was still but little more than a boy. Like all the Lees, he was public-spirited and patriotic and thoroughly loyal to his brilliant brother, Richard Henry, whom he supported in every measure which that able and far-seeing statesman held for the good of either his native Province or the Colonies at large.

The family of Rebecca Tayloe Lee dated back to Hon. William Taylor, of London, who came to Virginia in the seventeenth century and accumulated a fortune. In 1650, we find him buying large holdings of land in Lancaster and Richmond counties. It is not known when or by whom the change was made in the spelling of the name, from Taylor to Tayloe. He married Ann Corbin, daughter of Hon. Henry and Alice Eltonhead Corbin of "Buckingham House," Middlesex County, and had four children, one of which died in childhood. Two of the children were twins, John and Elizabeth. Elizabeth married Colonel Richard Corbin of King and Queen County, and John, the founder of "Mt. Airy," married Rebecca Plater of St. Mary's County, Maryland. "Mt. Airy" was built, in 1758, of red sandstone and white marble, and consisted of "a vast central building of fine proportions, with right and left wings joined by semicircular corridors. The portraits of Mt. Airy are considered one of the finest collections in America." John Taylor (or Tayloe) was an influential member of the King's Council under Lord Dunmore. He was the father of eleven children, nearly all of whom grew up and married into other of the old families of Virginia.

Francis Lightfoot Lee and his wife lived on his estate "Manokin," Richmond County, from their marriage in 1769 until their deaths in 1797, she dying in January and he following her in February. They had no children.

Judith Robinson Braxton

Judith Robinson, the first wife of Carter Braxton of King William County. came from a family highly prominent in the Old Dominion, from the time of its founding by Col. Christopher Robinson, who came to Virginia in 1666. He was a brother of the Rt. Rev. John Robinson, D.D., Lord Bishop of London during the reign of Queen Anne. Col. Robinson settled in Middlesex County, calling his estate "Hewick," and was one of the original trustees of William and Mary College, a member of the House of Burgesses, and a member of the King's Council. John Robinson, father of Judith, was a grandson of the original Christopher of Hewick, and his wife was the daughter of Hon. John Wormley.

Judith Robinson was married to Carter Braxton in 1755, and went to live on his estate "Elsing Green," King William County. We know but little of the personality of the first Mrs. Braxton or her successor, save from the brief information gleaned from the family genealogies and Bishop Meade's *Old Families of Virginia.* These show that to Carter Braxton and his wife Judith Robinson there were born children as follows: Mary Braxton, who married Robert Page of "Broadnech House," Hanover County, in 1779; and Judith Braxton, who married the same year John White of King William County, a son of Rev. Alexander White, rector of St. David's Parish. The girl mother died shortly after the birth of her second daughter in 1757, in the twenty-first year of her age—the same age as the young husband who survived her.

Elizabeth Corbin Braxton

Four years after the death of his first wife, Mr. Braxton married Elizabeth Corbin of "Laneville," King and Queen County, daughter of Colonel Richard and Elizabeth Tayloe Corbin, a family dating back to 1650 when Hon. Henry Corbin came from England and established "Buckingham House," in Middlesex County. Colonel Richard, grandson of "Henry, of Buckingham House," received his education in England and was a devoted churchman (Episcopal). Bishop Meade tells of his furnishing gratuitously the bread and wine for the communion and boarding the unmarried ministers who served the parish, without charge. He was President of the King's Council and Receiver General of the Colony. By his second wife Carter Braxton had sixteen children, several of whom died in infancy or early childhood. Elizabeth, the eldest child of Elizabeth Corbin Braxton, married Colonel Samuel Griffin, who served in the Revolution and afterward was a member of Congress; Carter, of King William County, who married a "Miss Sayre, granddaughter of Hon. Philip Ludwell"; and Colonel George Braxton, of "Chericoke," who married Mary, daughter of Hon. Charles and Mary Carter Carter of "Shirley," Charles City County. Mr. Braxton was a member of the House of Burgesses as early as 1765, and began taking an active part in Colonial matters, and, being a man of considerable force of character and personal influence, acquired such prominence that upon the death of Peyton Randolph, in 1775, he was elected as his successor in the Continental Congress.

Anne Clark Hooper

Anne Clark, daughter of Thomas Clark, Esq., and sister of Thomas Clark, Jr., afterward General of the U. S. Army, was married in 1767 to William Hooper, a brilliant young lawyer from Boston, who, after graduating from Harvard, studying law with James Otis, and visiting the South for some months, had decided to locate in Wilmington, N. C., and establish a practice. Of his bride it was written: "His choice was most fortunate, considered in reference to the qualifications of the lady to adorn and sweeten social and domestic life. It was most fortunate, too, considered in reference to that firmness of mind which enabled her to sustain without repining the grievous privations and distresses to which she became peculiarly exposed in consequence of the prominent station which Mr. Hooper held in the War of the Revolution."

But there were other dangers that the young lawyer had to face before he had become obnoxious to the British authorities. A paper written for Wheeler's *History of North Carolina*, by a Mr. Heart of Hillsborough, in the early part of the last century, throws a side-light on some of these dangers as well as giving an interesting picture of the times:

"His life was very strenuous at this time, the distance between the courts being great and the roads being poor; also the hospitality of his friends was trying to his health. Times were prosperous, and the dissipation which arose out of an excess of hospitality exhibited an even more animated picture in the surrounding country. Whole families and sometimes several families together were in the practice of making visits, and, like the tents of the Arabs, seemed continually on the move. The number of visitants, the noise and bustle of arriving and greeting, the cries of the poultry yard, and the bleatings from the pasture would require some sounding polysyllables to convey an idea of the joyous uproar. . . . Every visit was a sort of jubilee. Festive entertainment, balls, every species of amusement which song and dance could afford, were resorted to. The sports of the turf and the pleasure of the chase were alternately the objects of eager pursuit. Everywhere on the eastern and western branches of the Cape Fear River were men of fortune, related to one another by blood or marriage, whose settlements extended almost as far as the lowlands of Crossneck."

It was among these hospitable, happy-go-lucky, fox-chasing, horse-racing planters that young Hooper travelled from court to court, spending a week or so in a place, working assiduously for his clients by day and being "entertained" much of his time out of court. It was a lucrative practice and he accumulated money, but it was trying upon his frail constitution.

It was natural that he should almost at once be drawn into politics. In 1773, he was elected to the Legislature, and, the year following, was sent as a delegate to the Congress of 1774 and continued in '75, '76, and '77, but was granted leave of absence early in '77 to return to North Carolina and look after his family.

Mr. Hooper had left his wife and children in Wilmington when he first went to Congress, but, because of his activities and especially after he signed the Declaration, the British became very offensive. His property was destroyed on frequent occasions; a British captain went out of his way to sail up the Cape Fear River about three miles from Wilmington and shell a house belonging to Mr. Hooper. The brutal David Fanning who raided Hillsborough treated Mrs. Hooper and her family with rudeness amounting to downright cruelty. Mrs. Hooper had moved her family from Wilmington back to their plantation, about eight miles, but even there they were constantly harassed, and finally Mr. Hooper brought them back to Wilmington, and after the evacuation of that city took up his permanent residence at Hillsborough.

His health was badly broken, however, and he was compelled to give up most of his practice and other duties in 1778, while his wife looked after their plantation very successfully. Mr. Hooper died in 1790, leaving the widow to care for their three children, two sons and one daughter. The daughter, Elizabeth, married a business man of Hillsborough, named Watters. William Hooper, the eldest son, married and had several children who became prominent, especially one of them, Rev. William Hooper, Professor of Languages in the North Carolina University and a writer of some note.[19]

Susan Lyme Penn

Susan Lyme, one of the least known of the wives of the signers, was born in Kent County, Va., in 1741 or '42, and married to John Penn in 1763. Her husband was a young lawyer who had had to rely largely upon his own exertions to prepare for the honoured career he had before him.

Mr. Penn was a son of Moses and Catherine Taylor Penn, farming people of Caroline County. The elder Penn was prosperous but very neglectful of the young man's educational advantages, and when Moses Penn died in 1759 his son found himself sole heir to a fair property but had never had more than two or three terms of schooling. He was a cousin of Edmund Pendleton, a man of wealth and education, who opened his home and library to his young kinsman, who made so good use of his opportunities that at the age of twenty-one he was admitted to the bar with considerable reputation for vigorous eloquence. He removed to North Carolina in 1774, and soon established a practice. Almost from the first he became a leader, being sent to Congress in 1775 and kept there for several years, as well as receiving other high honours.

Three children were born to Susan and John Penn, only one of whom came to maturity. That was their only daughter, Lucy, who married Hon. John Taylor of Caroline County, Va., a planter who is said to have done much to advance the science of agriculture in his native State. He was colonel of cavalry in the Virginia line during the Revolution and elected to succeed Richard

Henry Lee in the U. S. Senate in 1792, but resigned in 1794. He was again sent to the Senate in 1803 to fill a vacancy. Taylor County, Virginia, was named in his honour, and General Zachary Taylor came of the same family. John Penn died in 1788, in his forty-seventh year. His wife survived him many years.

Henrietta Middleton Rutledge

Henrietta Middleton, who married Edward Rutledge, afterward member of the Continental Congress and Governor of South Carolina, was a noted woman of a notable family. She was a daughter of Henry Middleton, President of the Provincial Council and afterward of the Continental Congress. He was probably the largest landowner in South Carolina, having over 50,000 acres, twenty plantations, and 800 slaves. She was born in Charleston in 1750 and married at the age of twenty-four to the brilliant young lawyer, Edward Rutledge, still fresh from completing his legal education in England.

Mrs. Rutledge's mother was Mary Williams. On the tomb at Middleton Place on the Ashley river, near Charleston, is this inscription: "Underneath this stone is deposited Mary

Middleton, a sincere Christian. She was the only child of John Williams and the beloved wife of Henry Middleton with whom she lived near twenty years in unreserved confidence. Two sons and five daughters lived to lament her. She departed this life Jan. 9th, 1761, in the forty-sixth year of her age.—Much beloved and much lamented."

Mrs. Rutledge fell into ill health soon after her marriage, lived quietly, and took no part in social or political life. Possessed of great wealth in her own right, the wife of the most successful lawyer in the State and well fitted by birth and education to grace any society, she had not the physical strength and died in 1792, leaving two children, a son, Henry Middleton Rutledge, afterward a prominent citizen of Tennessee, and a daughter, Sarah, who never married.

Some time after the death of his first wife, Col. Rutledge was married to his first love, Mary Shubrick, widow of Col. Nicholas Eveleigh, formerly Comptroller of the U. S. Treasury by appointment of President Washington. Thomas Shubrick had opposed the suit of Edward Rutledge when the young man first desired to pay court to his daughter, and old Andrew Rutledge, his father, refused to allow his son to pay his addresses to Miss Shubrick. The young people obediently married to please their parents, as was largely the custom in those days, but remained friends. When Providence removed the wife of one and the husband of the other in the same year, it was not long until they came together and were married, and, it is said, lived most happily. No children were born of this second marriage, but the second Mrs. Rutledge is said to have been a devoted step-mother and friend to Sarah Rutledge, and the two lived together after Governor Rutledge's death, devoting much of their time to caring for the poor and friendless and other charitable work. To this work Sarah Rutledge practically gave up her life, caring especially for orphan and homeless girls, and looking after their maintenance and education.

Elizabeth Mathews Heyward

Elizabeth Mathews, a sister of Governor John Mathews of South Carolina, was the first wife of Col. Thomas Heyward. The date of their marriage is not definitely known, but it was about 1767 or '68—just after he returned from a several years' stay in Europe, where his father, Col. Daniel Heyward, a wealthy planter, had sent him to complete his education, by study and travel. The young man came back an enthusiastic American and an ardent patriot, and became an active participant in both the Continental Congress to which he was elected in 1775, and in the field. He was shot through the leg and taken prisoner during the siege of Charleston, and carried to the British prison at St. Augustine, where he was kept nearly a year. During this time a detachment was sent to plunder his plantation. His family were forced to fly for their lives, their home was looted, and nearly two hundred slaves carried away and sent to Jamaica and sold. His loss from the slaves alone was estimated at upwards of $50,-000. The shock of this experience was one from which Mrs. Heyward never recovered and she died in 1781, about the time that he was released by exchange. She was the mother of five children, all of whom died in infancy except her son Daniel.

Col. Heyward married, as his second wife, Miss Elizabeth Savage, by whom he had three children. He died in the sixty-third year of his

age, in 1809, and was survived by his widow and
four children, as follows: Daniel, the son of the
first wife, was married to Anne Sarah Trezevant,
and their daughter Elizabeth married Captain
James Hamilton, U. S. Army, who afterward
became a member of Congress and, in 1830,
Governor of South Carolina. He was brigadier-
general of militia and in command during the
Nullification excitement in 1832 and '33. He
afterward removed to Texas and represented
that young republic at the Court of St. James's
in 1841. He was drowned at the time of the
collision of the *Opelousa* and *Galveston* off the
coast of Texas, after giving up his life preserver
to a lady.

The three children born to Col. Heyward by
his second wife were: Thomas, who married
Ann Elisa Cutbert; James Hamilton, who married Decima Shubrick, sister of Rear Admiral
William Branford Shubrick, U. S. N.; and Elizabeth Savage, who married Henry Middleton
Parker.

Elizabeth Shubrick Lynch

Elizabeth Shubrick, the beautiful girl who in
1773 married the sweetheart of her girlhood days,

was destined to add another chapter to the tragic story of the Carolina signers and their families.

Thomas Lynch, Jr., son of a wealthy planter of St. George Parish, after eight years in England in which he had prepared at Eton, taken his degree at Cambridge, and read law at The Temple, returned home in 1772 determined to devote his life to advancing the best interests of his country, a resolution directly in line with the wishes of his father. He married Elizabeth Shubrick, daughter of an old and prominent family, and they took up their residence on a plantation which the elder Lynch had given them. In 1774 he became a captain of militia and a year later was elected member of Congress to fill a vacancy caused by the breaking down of the health of his father. His own health had been seriously impaired by a fever he had acquired by a term of recruiting service which he had undertaken. However, he attended Congress, signed the Declaration, which he and his father both heartily favoured, and then, his health still failing, decided to act on the advice of his physicians and friends and take a voyage to the south of Europe. He and his young wife sailed to the West Indies in 1779, to secure passage on some neutral vessel, and were never heard from again. It is supposed the ship went down and that Thomas Lynch and his wife perished with all on board.

Mary Izard Middleton

Mary Izard, daughter of Col. Walter Izard of Cedar Grove, an officer of the Provincial militia, and Elizabeth Gibbs, his wife, was said to have been one of the most beautiful and accomplished young women of her day in South Carolina. She was married in 1764 to Hon. Arthur Middleton, brother of Mrs. Edward Rutledge and son of Hon. Henry Middleton of The Oaks and Middleton Place. She died in 1814, half a century after her marriage with the young patriot and statesman and twenty-seven years after her husband, who died on his plantation near Charleston in 1787. A portrait of Mrs. Middleton and her husband and eldest son was painted by Benjamin West in London, during the year or two Mrs. Middleton and her husband spent in travelling before the Revolution. This picture now hangs at Alverthorpe, near Philadelphia, the country home of her great-grandson,

Dr. Henry Middleton Fisher. One of her great-great-grand daughters is in possession of a miniature of Mrs. Middleton set in rubies and diamonds. Both pictures show an aristocratic, high-bred face with arched eyebrows, dark hair, white skin, and slender throat. The *Courier* of Charleston, July, 1814, has this notice: "Died at her residence in Mazyckborough, Mrs. Mary Middleton, relict of that distinguished patriot, the late Hon. Arthur Middleton, Esq. This excellent woman has descended to the tomb endeared to society by her Virtues and her good works."

The Middletons suffered severely from the war. His biographer tells of some instances which show not only the patriotism of Mrs. Middleton but of her husband's serene philosophy: "During the Revolution when Governor Rutledge needed help in 1779, when Provost was trying to reduce Charleston, many of the patriots whose family seats lay in the route of the British, hastened home to save their property, Mr. Middleton merely sent word to his wife to remove to the house of a friend a day's journey north of Charleston. The buildings at Middleton Place were spared but house and barns rifled.

Everything that could not be converted into lucrative purpose was demolished. Pictures were slashed and frames broken.

"During the war, 200 slaves were carried away and he had become deeply in debt, but with his uncomplaining wife he passed several years in unceasing struggles, yet with generous hospitality.

"The house he occupied on the Ashley, while large and commodious, did not altogether correspond with the appearance of two more modern wings. Mr. Middleton sometimes talked of taking it down and building on another plan, but friends dissuaded him because it was too large a superstructure to sacrifice to any plan of improvement. When one day he was out walking, Mrs. Middleton sent a servant to tell him the house was on fire. Looking around and seeing that the atmosphere was calm and that the two wings were not in danger, he sent back, saying, 'Let it burn.' Mrs. Middleton did not view the matter so coolly and soon had the fire extinguished."

Mrs. Middleton was the mother of nine children, three sons and six daughters. Her eldest son, Henry Middleton, was successively a member of both branches of the Legislature and Governor of his own State, member of Congress and Minister to the Court of St. Petersburg. He married Mary Helen Hering, daughter of Julius Hering of Heybridge Hall, Captain in H. M. 34th Regiment. John Izard Middleton, the second son, of Cedar Grove, received his mother's large fo⁻tune. He spent most of his life in France and Italy and was devoted to art. He was an amateur painter of talent and author of the book *Grecian Remains in Italy*. He married Elisa Augusta, daughter of Theodore de Palazieu Falconet. John the third son died in infancy, in 1787. Maria Henrietta, the oldest daughter, born 1772, married Joseph Manigault; Elisa Carolina, the second, born in 1774, died unmarried; Emma Philadelphia, born in 1776, married Henry Izard, eldest son of Hon. Ralph Izard, U. S. Senator; Anne Louise born 1778, married Daniel Blake; Isabella Johannes, born 1780, married Hon. Daniel Elliott Huger, U. S. Senator for South Carolina; Septima Sexta, born 1783, married Henry Middleton Rutledge.

Mrs. Button Gwinnett

But little has come down to us of Mrs. Button Gwinnett,[20] wife of that unfortunate English-

man who, coming to Georgia in 1773, was elected
a delegate to the Continental Congress in 1775,
'76, and '77, and then President of the Council,
the highest office of the Province. We know that
she was a wife and mother when they came from
Bristol, England, to South Carolina in 1770.
We know that the Gwinnetts spent two years in
the mercantile business in Charleston and that
then Mr. Gwinnett paid £5250 for a tract of
land in Georgia on St. Catharine Island, "including a stock of horses, cattle, and hogs, some
lumber and a plantation boat." We know that
she went to live on this island with her children,
and that is about all that has been told.

Until 1777, Gwinnett's rise had been phenome-
nal. Converted from his natural Tory principles
by Dr. Lyman Hall, he entered with all the ardour
of his positive, determined nature into the
struggle for independence—going farther, even,
than a majority of the native Georgia leaders.
But the tide of his popularity turned. He made
enemies and excited jealousies. He was defeated in the selection of a brigadier-general for
a brigade of troops which Georgia was required
to raise for the Continental Army, and afterward
for Governor. Growing out of these defeats

came the quarrel with Col. Lachlan McIntosh, and the duel which resulted fatally for Gwinnett. All we know of Mrs. Gwinnett at that time is that she nursed him during the twelve days he lay groaning with his shattered hip, and then she and her children drop out of all knowledge, and the chroniclers of the day who mention her simply say that "Mrs. Gwinnett and her children soon followed him."

Abigail Burr Hall

Abigail Burr, the beautiful and accomplished daughter of Thaddeus Burr, Esq., of Wallingford, Conn., became the wife of Dr. Lyman Hall in May, 1752, and was borne to an untimely grave in July of the following year.

In 1757 or thereabouts, Dr. Hall, having been married the second time to Mary Osborne, removed to Dorchester, South Carolina,²¹ and a few months later to Georgia, where he made his home and established a practice in the town of Sunbury, St. John's Parish. He also purchased and cultivated a rice plantation a few miles from Midway, on the Savannah road. He became one of the leading physicians of the Province and highly prosperous. Naturally he came to have a great deal of influence in his section of the country and was the leader of the patriotic faction that finally forced Georgia to join her sister Colonies in enacting the Declaration of Independence, and was one of the five representatives sent by the Provincial Assembly to represent Georgia in the Continental Congress. One of these representatives was opposed to the Declaration and did not attend, and another, Archibald Bulloch, though a decided patriot, was unable to leave Georgia at the time, thus leaving only Gwinnett, Hall, and Walton to sign the Declaration. When the British took possession of Georgia, Mr. Hall, took his family north for safety and left his residence unprotected. His property was confiscated. He was Governor of Georgia in 1782, after which he retired to a home in Burke County, where he died in 1790 in his sixtieth year. His only son had died a few years before, but Mrs. Hall survived him several years.

A monument has been erected to the memory of Lyman Hall in his native town of Wallingford, Conn. Upon a mound of earth, handsomely turfed, is a large flat freestone, nearly nine feet long by six feet wide. Upon this rests a block of freestone, nearly three feet high, with rounded corners and handsome mouldings; on the fourth side of which is this inscription: "The State of Georgia having removed to Augusta, the remains of Lyman Hall, a signer of the Declaration of Independence, and there erected a monument to his memory, the original tablet covering his grave was, in 1857, presented by William D'Antignac to this State, by whose order it is deposited in his native town."

Inscribed upon the tablet, which is of white marble about three inches thick, is the following:

"Beneath this stone rest the remains of the Hon. Lyman Hall, Formerly Governor of this State, who departed this life the 19th of Oct., 1790, in the 67th year of his age.

"In the cause of America he was uniformly a patriot. In the incumbent duties of a husband and a father he acquitted himself with affection and tenderness. But, reader, above all, know from this inscription that he left the probationary scene as a true Christian and an honest man.

"To those so mourned in death, so loved in life,
The childless parent, the widowed wife,
With tears inscribes this monumental stone
That holds his ashes and expects her own."

This poetical epitaph was written by Mrs. Hall, who died childless, their son, who died a few years before his father, being their only child.

Dorothy Camber Walton

Dorothy Camber, who became the wife of George Walton, the young patriot and signer of the Declaration of Independence, was the daughter of an English gentleman residing in Chatham County, Ga. Like the wives of the other signers from Georgia we have little record of the young woman's personality. A year after their marriage we find Col. Walton leading his regiment in defence of Savannah, where he was desperately wounded and taken prisoner. Gen. Robert Howe, under whose command he was fighting, wrote him a letter of sympathy and commending his bravery. He was sent to Sunbury and held as prisoner. Because of his being a member of Congress and a signer, the British refused to exchange him for any one of less rank than a brigadier-general. It was from this prison, when it was thought that his wound would prove fatal, that he wrote to his wife:

"Remember that you are the beloved wife of

one who has made honour and reputation the ruling motive in every action of his life."

Mr. Walton who began life as a carpenter's apprentice in his native city of Fredericksburg, Va., had by sheer force of character and native ability, been elected to Congress six times; was twice Governor of his adopted State, once a Senator of the United States, and for fifteen years a judge of the Superior Courts. He never accumulated property, but he and his wife lived contentedly on their little farm near Augusta. They had but one son, who bore his father's name and served as Secretary of State during the time Andrew Jackson was Governor of West Florida. George Walton died in 1804 and was buried in Augusta. His wife survived him several years.

NOTES TO CHAPTER II

[1] Most of the facts given in this connection are from an address by Charles Henry Hart, Esq., on the life of Mrs. Morris, made in June, 1877, and an article in the Pennsylvania *Historical Magazine*, on the unpublished manuscripts of Robert Morris, by Henry Holmes, LL.D.

[2] Mr. John Calvert, Philadelphia.

[3] Few American families have more prominent men and women among their descendants than that of Richard Bache and Sarah Franklin. Three of the present generation are Miss Alice Irwin, LL.D., head of Radcliffe College, Cambridge, Mass.; Richard Wainwright, U. S. N., executive officer of the battleship *Maine*, at the time she was blown up in Havana harbour, and in command of the

Gloucester in the battle off Santiago in 1898; and Rene Bache, a well-known journalist of Washington, D.C.

⁴ Reese Meredith and George Washington were personal friends long before the Revolution. Their acquaintance is said to have come about in this way: Mr. Meredith was lunching at an inn in Philadelphia, and fell into conversation with a tall young Virginian, over some venison that had been served. They became mutually interested and, before separating, Mr. Meredith had invited the young man to his home, to discuss a haunch of venison which had been sent to him. Washington accepted and the friendship then formed was never broken.

⁵ Charles W. Stewart, a graduate of Annapolis (Class of '81), who is in charge of the naval war records at the Navy Department, and regarded as one of the greatest students in the government service, is a direct descendant of James Smith, the Signer. The Class of '81 was prevented from entering upon the work for which they had been trained, by a special act of Congress, because of an over-abundance of naval officers.

⁶ George Taylor's will, which was proved March 10, 1781, refers to five grandchildren, George, Thomas, James, Ann, and Mary. He is also known to have had a child by his housekeeper, Naomi Smith.

⁷ Portraits of both George Ross and Ann Lawlor Ross were painted by Benjamin West, some time between 1755 and 1760 and are in possession of a lineal descendant, Mr. George Eshelman of Lancaster, Pa.

⁸ Cæsar Rodney, the first of Delaware's signers of the Declaration of Independence, was never married. The late Thomas F. Bayard, in an oration pronounced at the unveiling of a monument to Cæsar Rodney erected at Dover in 1889, said: "Cæsar Rodney never married, and the happiness of conjugal life, which he was so fitted by his amiable disposition to enjoy, was denied him. There are certain confidences so purely personal that the right to have them maintained survives. Mr. Rodney was too warm-hearted a man not to have cherished an attachment warmer and stronger than friendship. Among his papers proof of such dedication of his love and devotion have been found, but it was not his happy fate to form the union which his heart desired."

⁹ This date is erroneously given as 1762, in Sanderson's *Lives of the Signers*.

¹⁰ In a letter to John Adams, dated November 8, 1779, Mr.

McKean writes: "I have had my full share of the anxieties, cares, and troubles of the present war. For some time I was obliged to act as President of Delaware State, and as chief justice of this (Pennsylvania). General Howe had just landed (August, 1777) at the head of Elk River, when I undertook to discharge these two important trusts. The consequence was, to be hunted like a fox by the enemy, and envied by those who ought to have been my friends. I was compelled to remove my family five times in a few months, and at last fixed them in a little log house on the banks of the Susquehanna, more than a hundred miles from this place; but safety was not to be found there, for they were soon obliged to move again on account of the incursions of the Indians."

¹¹ Sarah McKean, eldest daughter of Governor McKean by his second wife, Sarah Armitage, and familiarly known as "Miss Sally McKean," was a famous belle in Philadelphia society, while that city was the seat of the national government. She was married in 1798 to Senor Don Carlos Martinez de Yrujo, Spanish Minister to the United States, 1796 to 1807; ennobled, 1803, and created Marquis de Casa Yrujo; became obnoxious to President and Cabinet by opposition to the Louisiana Purchase and his recall was requested. Later he was Minister to Brazil until 1813, when he became Minister of Spain at Paris; later was Secretary of Foreign Affairs until his death in Madrid in January, 1824. His widow, known after her marriage as Sarah Maria Theresa, Marchioness de Casa Yrujo, died in Madrid in January, 1841.

¹² Samuel Chase, Jr., second son of Judge Chase, the Signer, became a judge in the District of Columbia; William Pinckney, whom he took into his own home and educated, became Attorney-General, and held several other high positions.

¹³ In the *National Cyclopedia of American Biography* it is stated that "One of Governor Paca's daughters was married to Consul Roubelle, a coadjutor of Napoleon. Their son bore such a striking likeness to the accepted ideals of our Saviour that he was often called upon to pose as a model." Other authorities agree that John P. Paca was the only surviving child.

In her *Colonial Families*, Mary Burke Emory makes the statement that "Mrs. William Paca's second husband was Daniel Dulaney. They had two sons, Floyd, who was pierced with a sword in a duel with Rev. Bennett Allen, and Walter Dulaney." All other authorities seem to agree that both of Governor Paca's wives died long before his decease.

[14] Hon. John Lee Carroll, the present representative of the family, was elected Governor of Maryland just a century after the Declaration of Independence and filled the Executive chair until 1880. He lives on the ancestral estate and bids fair to reach the age of " Carroll of Carrollton," who died at ninety-five.

[15] Thomas Lee, grandson of Richard Lee, the founder of the family in America, was for many years President of the Council of Virginia. He married Hannah Ludwell, sister of Col. Ludwell, a member of the Council. The offspring of this union are particularly celebrated in the annals of America. They were: (1) Philip Ludwell, a member of the Council of State, who died about the beginning of the Revolution; (2) Thomas Ludwell, a judge of the Supreme Court, and member of Assembly, died early in the Revolution; (3) Francis Lightfoot, member of the Continental Congress and signer of the Declaration; Richard Henry, orator and statesman, "was a member of the first American Congress in 1774, was the author of the masterly second address of Congress to the people of Great Britain, and in a great burst of eloquence proposed to Congress on June 7, 1776, the Declaration of Independence"; William, Minister at The Hague, Vienna, and Berlin; Arthur, diplomatist and statesman and author.

A son of a cousin of the six brothers was Henry Lee, "Light-horse Harry" as he came to be called during the Revolution, in which he was an able and dashing cavalry officer. He was elected a member of Congress in 1786, and pronounced the famous eulogy over Washington: "First in War, first in Peace, and first in the hearts of his countrymen." He married Lucy Grymes. General Robert E. Lee, Confederate General and afterward President of William and Mary College, was son of General Henry Lee. The late Gen. Fitzhugh Lee, of the Spanish-American War, was of the same descent.

[16] Lieutenant William Taylor Smith, U. S. N., is a descendant of Thomas Jefferson, on his mother's side. His father, Edward Jaqueline Smith of Edgeville, Va., traces his ancestry back to Sir Thomas Smith, a brother of Captain John Smith of Jamestown.

[17] Two descendants of Benjamin Harrison are members of the National House of Representatives, Hon. Francis Burton Harrison of New York and Hon. Byran Patton Harrison of Mississippi. The Carter Harrisons, father and son, several times mayors of Chicago, are descendants of Benjamin Harrison the Signer.

[18] Thomas Nelson Page, the well-known and popular writer, is a direct descendant of Governor Thomas Nelson, the Signer.

[19] Joseph Hewes died unmarried in 1779. He was affianced to Isabella Johnson, sister of Governor Johnson, and with her sister Mrs. Hannah Iredel a signer of the famous "Edenton Compact." She died early in 1779 and Mr. Hewes, who was deeply attached to her, survived only a few months.

[20] When Georgia's capital was captured by the British in 1778, all the public records and many private papers stored there for safe keeping were destroyed. In consequence of this much authentic data concerning the three Signers and their families has been lost.

[21] The South Carolina *Historical and Genealogical Magazine* (vol., iii.) reprints the following from the South Carolina *Gazette* of July 24, 1777. "The subscriber, practitioner in physic and surgery, having removed to Ponpon, would hereby acquaint his friends and others, that he will be ready at all hours to serve them in his profession and doubts not of giving satisfaction. He has also to sell, a good assortment of family MEDECINES, perfumery waters and other medecaments, and continues to make and sell a famous cosmetic water for the ladies, which may also be had at Mr. John Wilmer's, in Church Street, Charles-Town."

"LYMAN HALL."

NOTES

NOTES

WallBuilders Resources

P.O. Box 397 • Aledo, TX 76008 • To place a MasterCard or Visa order, call

1-800-873-2845

Prices subject to change without notice. Quantity & case-lot discounts available.

Videos

America's Godly Heritage (60 min.)   **(V01) $19.95**
Explains the Founding Fathers' beliefs concerning the role of Christian principles in the public affairs of the nation.

Education and the Founding Fathers (60 min.)   **(V02) $19.95**
A look at the educational system which produced America's great heroes.

Foundations of American Government (25 min.)   **(V03) $9.95**
Surveys the historical statements and records surrounding the drafting of the First Amendment, showing the Founders' intent.

Keys to Good Government (59 min.)   **(V05) $19.95**
Presents beliefs of the Founders concerning the proper role of Biblical thinking in education, government, and public affairs.

Spirit of the American Revolution (53 min.)   **(V04) $19.95**
A look at the motivation that caused the Founders to pledge their "lives, fortunes, and sacred honor" to establish our nation.

The Spiritual Heritage of the U.S. Capitol (2 hours)   **(V06) $39.00***
A personal tour of the U.S. Capitol with WallBuilders founder David Barton complete with dramatic reenactments. *Donation (Do not add sales tax and shipping.)

Books

America: To Pray or Not to Pray   **(B01A) $7.95**
A statistical look at what has happened when religious principles were separated from public affairs by the Supreme Court in 1962.

Benjamin Rush: Hardback **(B20A) $15.95**
Signer of the Declaration of Independence   Paperback **(B20) $9.95**
Features the life and writings of this dedicated Christian statesman, including numerous historical illustrations.

The Bulletproof George Washington   **(B05) $6.95**
An account of God's miraculous protection of Washington in the French and Indian War and of Washington's open gratitude for God's Divine intervention.

Bible Study Course – New Testament   **(B09) $4.95**
A reprint of the 1946 N.T. survey text used by the Dallas Public High Schools.

Bible Study Course – Old Testament   **(B12) $4.95**
A reprint of the 1954 O.T. survey text used by the Dallas Public High Schools.

A Constitutional Amendment Protecting School Prayer & Religious Speech **(B27) $3.95**
Religious liberties can be restored and protected through the new "Religious Speech Amendment" to the Constitution. Read the objections and responses.

Documents of Freedom (B21) $3.95
Pocket-size copy of the Declaration of Independence, the U.S. Constitution, and George Washington's Farewell Address.

Ethics: An Early American Handbook (B23) $7.95
An historical reprint of an 1890 textbook that taught character to America's young people. Great for all ages!

Impeachment! Restraining an Overactive Judiciary (B17) $6.95
This book reveals how the Founders restrained overactive courts via impeachment. Learn how we can do the same with our judges today.

Lessons From Nature for Youth (B13A) $6.95
This 1836 reprint will teach young people admirable traits once taught in our schools. Learn loyalty from a buffalo, gratitude from a lion, etc. Great for all ages!

Lives of the Signers of the Declaration of Independence (B14A) $10.95
This reprint of an 1848 original features biographic sketches on the lives of each of the 56 men who signed the Declaration of Independence.

The New England Primer (B06) $6.95
A reprint of the 1777 textbook used by the Founding Fathers. It was the first textbook printed in America (1690) and was used for 200 years to teach reading and Bible lessons in school.

Original Intent Hardback (B24) $19.95 • Paperback (B16) $12.95
Reveals how the Court has reinterpreted the Constitution, diluting the principles upon which it was based. Allows the Founders to speak for themselves.

The Practical Benefits of Christianity (B26) $3.95
Demonstrates the positive and powerful societal influences which the Founding Fathers believed Christianity provided.

The Second Amendment (B25) $5.95
Read the Founders' words and examine their early laws on the Second Amendment. Learn of their proposals on how to deal with gun violence.

A Spiritual Heritage Tour of the U.S. Capitol (B22) $6.95
A self-guided tour of the U.S. Capitol Building which focuses on the Godly heritage found in artwork, statues, etc., throughout the building.

Webster's "Advice to the Young" (B10A) $6.95
Founder Noah Webster stated that this work "will be useful in enlightening the minds of youth in religious and moral principles."

Wives of the Signers (B18A) $10.95
This reprint describes those women who, alongside their husbands, experienced the struggle for independence and the building of a new nation.

Video Transcripts

America's Godly Heritage (See video)	(TSC01) $3.95
Education and the Founding Fathers (See video)	(TSC02) $3.95
Foundations of American Government (See video)	(TSC03) $2.95
Keys to Good Government (See video)	(TSC04) $3.95
Spirit of the American Revolution (See video)	(TSC05) $3.95

Historic Print

The Battle of Lexington   **(PR01) $24.95**
Framable, museum-quality print of the Battle of Lexington by W.B. Wollen (18 x 24).

American Heritage Poster Series

A series of posters designed to give an enjoyable overview of great men, women, and events in America's history. These beautiful 16 x 20 informational posters are excellent for use in schools or homeschool classrooms.

Abraham Lincoln	**(P04) $4.95**
First Prayer in Congress	**(P07) $4.95**
First Thanksgiving	**(P08) $4.95**
George Washington	**(P06) $4.95**
George Washington Carver	**(P02) $4.95**
Pocahontas	**(P05) $4.95**
The Signing of the Declaration of Independence	**(P10) $4.95**
Thomas Jefferson	**(P03) $4.95**
Any 5 Posters (write selections on order form)	**(PS5) $19.95**
Complete Poster Set (All 8 posters)	**(PS8) $27.95**

Authentic Historical Documents

Beautiful parchment replicas of significant documents which add an historical atmosphere to any classroom, home, or study

Bill of Rights	**(D02) $3.95**
Declaration of Independence	**(D01) $3.95**
Mayflower Compact of 1620	**(D04) $3.95**
Northwest Ordinance of 1787	**(D03) $3.95**
Patrick Henry's "Liberty or Death" Speech	**(D05) $3.95**
U.S. Constitution (4 pages)	**(D06) $9.95**

Compact Discs

America's Godly Heritage 1 & 2 (2-CD Set)   **(CD01) $13.95**
Learn the beliefs of the Founders on education, government, & public affairs.

Keys to Good Government plus
Faith, Character, & the Constitution (2-CD Set)   **(CD02) $13.95**
See video and audio cassette descriptions respectively for more information.

Moments From America's History   **(CD03) $8.95**
See description under Audio Cassettes.

The Spirit of the American Revolution
plus *America's Birthday (2-CD Set)*   **(CD04) $13.95**
See video and audio cassette descriptions respectively for more information.

The Spiritual Heritage of the U.S. Capitol (on 2 CDs)   **(CD05) $13.95**
See video and audio cassette descriptions respectively for more information.

Audio Cassettes

America's Birthday: The Fourth of July   (A20) $4.95
A fascinating look at our nation's birth and the great men and events involved in bringing us to the occasion.

America's Godly Heritage – Part One (See video)   (A01) $4.95

America's Godly Heritage – Part Two   (A15) $4.95
An expanded look at the Founding Fathers' beliefs concerning the role of Christian principles in the public affairs of the nation.

America: Lessons from Nehemiah   (A05) $4.95
A look at the Scriptural parallels between the rebuilding of Jerusalem in the book of Nehemiah and that of America today.

America: To Pray or Not To Pray? (See book)   (A07) $4.95

The Bible and the Judiciary   (A22) $4.95
Discover the role the Bible has historically played in America's courts and how it's been removed today.

The Changing First Amendment   (A19) $4.95
Shows how the courts have reinterpreted the First Amendment resulting in rulings opposed to the Founders' intent.

Developing a Biblical Worldview   (A28) $4.95
Insight on how to think like a Christian in every area of your life

Education and the Founding Fathers (See video)   (A08) $4.95

Faith and the Presidents   (A27) $4.95
Examines some of our chief executives and how they applied their faith

Faith, Character, and the Constitution   (A21) $4.95
Does character matter? Does religious faith have a part in today's society? Learn what the Founders believed on both issues.

Foundations of American Government (See video)   (A12) $4.95

The Founding Fathers   (A11) $4.95
Highlights accomplishments and notable quotes of Founding Fathers which show their strong belief in Christian principles.

Impeachment: Restraining an Overactive Judiciary (See book)   (A23) $4.95

The Importance of Duty   (A17) $4.95
Highlights how stewardship of rights and performance of responsibilities is the duty of each Christian.

Is America a Christian Nation?   (A16) $4.95
An examination of the writings of the Framers of the Constitution and of the Supreme Court's own records.

Keys to Good Government (See video)   (A09) $4.95

The Laws of the Heavens   **(A03) $4.95**
An explanation of the eight words in the Declaration of Independence on which the nation was birthed.

Moments From America's History   **(A24) $4.95**
The Founding Fathers on patriotism, national policy, religion, character, and voting – a series of one-minute commentaries.

The Practical Benefits of Christianity   **(A18) $4.95**
Demonstrates the positive and powerful societal influences which the Founding Fathers believed Christianity provided.

Principles for Reformation   **(A10) $4.95**
Explores the Biblical guidelines for restoring Christian principles to society and public affairs.

Religion & Morality, Indispensable Supports   **(A14) $4.95**
Documents the Founding Fathers' belief that religion and morality are indispensable supports for American society.

The Role of Pastors and Christians in Civil Government   **(A26) $4.95**
Discover the role that pastors and Christians played in the founding era and learn what you can do to have an impact today.

The Spirit of the American Revolution (See video)   **(A02) $4.95**

The Spiritual Heritage of the U.S. Capitol (See video) 2 audios   **(A25) $8.95**

Thinking Biblically, Speaking Secularly   **(A13) $4.95**
Provides guidelines for Biblically thinking individuals to effectively communicate truths in today's often anti-Biblical environment.

Pamphlets

America: God Shed His Grace on Thee **(25 count)**   **(PAM02) $2.95**
Gives quotes from the Founders highlighting their belief in government based upon Biblical principles.

The Bible in Schools **(25 count)**   **(PAM04) $3.95**
A reprint of an essay by Founding Father Benjamin Rush on why the Bible should be taught in schools.

Thanksgiving in America **(25 count)**   **(PAM07) $2.95**
The American Tract Society asked us to help them in preparing this tract with quotes from our Founding Fathers.

The Truth About Jefferson & the First Amendment   **(PAM01) $.50**
Explains a common misconception concerning Jefferson's role with the First Amendment and points out those who did influence it.

Order Form

Quan.	Code	Title	Unit Price	Total

Product Total	
S&H (see left)	
Sub-Total	
TX add 7.75%	
TOTAL	

Shipping & Handling

- When shipping to multiple addresses, calculate order minimum based on the dollar amount sent to each address, not on the order total.
- Add $1 to costs below for orders containing a poster, historical print, or historical document.
- Call for express shipping options and international shipping prices.

ORDER TOTAL	UPS RATE	POSTAL RATE
Under $5.00	5.00	4.50
$5.01 to 15.00	5.50	5.00
$15.01 to 25.00	6.50	5.50
$25.01 to 40.00	7.00	6.00
$40.01 to 60.00	7.50	6.50
$60.01 to 100.00	8.00	
Over $100.00	8%	

Please allow 4-6 weeks for delivery.

WallBuilders,
P.O. Box 397
Aledo, TX 76008
(817) 441-6044
www.wallbuilders.com

Mastercard/Visa orders call
1-800-873-2845 to order.